NEW DIRECTIONS FOR TEACHING AND LEARNING

Robert J. Menges, *Northwestern University*
EDITOR-IN-CHIEF

Marilla D. Svinicki, *University of Texas, Austin*
ASSOCIATE EDITOR

Using Active Learning in College Classes: A Range of Options for Faculty

Tracey E. Sutherland
Truman State University

Charles C. Bonwell
Saint Louis College of Pharmacy

EDITORS

Number 67, Fall 1996

JOSSEY-BASS PUBLISHERS
San Francisco

USING ACTIVE LEARNING IN COLLEGE CLASSES: A RANGE OF OPTIONS
FOR FACULTY
Tracey E. Sutherland, Charles C. Bonwell (eds.)
New Directions for Teaching and Learning, no. 67
Robert J. Menges, Editor-in-Chief
Marilla D. Svinicki, Associate Editor

Copyright © 1996 Jossey-Bass Inc., Publishers, 350 Sansome Street,
San Francisco, CA 94104.

Microfilm copies of issues and articles are available in 16mm and 35mm,
as well as microfiche in 105mm, through University Microfilms Inc., 300
North Zeeb Road, Ann Arbor, Michigan 48106-1346.

ISSN 0271-0633   ISBN 0-7879-9933-4

NEW DIRECTIONS FOR TEACHING AND LEARNING is part of The Jossey-Bass
Higher and Adult Education Series and is published quarterly by Jossey-
Bass Inc., Publishers, 350 Sansome Street, San Francisco, California
94104-1342. Second-class postage paid at San Francisco, California, and
at additional mailing offices. POSTMASTER: Send address changes to New
Directions for Teaching and Learning, Jossey-Bass Inc., Publishers, 350
Sansome Street, San Francisco, California 94104-1342.

SUBSCRIPTIONS cost $52.00 for individuals and $79.00 for institutions,
agencies, and libraries.

EDITORIAL CORRESPONDENCE should be sent to the editor-in-chief, Robert J.
Menges, Northwestern University, Center for the Teaching Professions,
2115 North Campus Drive, Evanston, Illinois 60208-2610.

Cover photograph by Richard Blair/Color & Light © 1990.

Manufactured in the United States of America on Lyons Falls
Pathfinder Tradebook. This paper is acid-free and 100 percent
totally chlorine-free.

Contents

98185

FROM THE SERIES EDITORS

About This Publication. Since 1980, *New Directions for Teaching and Learning* (NDTL) has brought a unique blend of theory, research, and practice to leaders in postsecondary education. *NDTL* sourcebooks strive not only for solid substance but also for timeliness, compactness, and accessibility.

The series has four goals: to inform readers about current and future directions in teaching and learning in postsecondary education, to illuminate the context that shapes these new directions, to illustrate these new directions through examples from real settings, and to propose ways in which these new directions can be incorporated into still other settings.

This publication reflects our view that teaching deserves respect as a high form of scholarship. We believe that significant scholarship is conducted not only by researchers who report results of empirical investigations but also by practitioners who share disciplined reflections about teaching. Contributors to *NDTL* approach questions of teaching and learning as seriously as they approach substantive questions in their own disciplines, and they deal not only with pedagogical issues but also with the intellectual and social context in which these issues arise. Authors deal on the one hand with theory and research and on the other with practice, and they translate from research and theory to practice and back again.

About This Volume. In this volume the authors take a second look at the use of active learning in higher education. The chapters describe the concept of the active learning continuum and tie various practical examples of active learning to that concept. They illustrate how important it is to consider context in the design of active learning to get maximum benefit.

Robert J. Menges, *Editor-in-Chief*
Marilla D. Svinicki, *Associate Editor*

EDITORS' NOTES

We began this project with the strong conviction that active learning is necessary for achieving many course objectives, and that all faculty can and should use it in their teaching. However, through our day-to-day work with faculty we have also become concerned that many instructors think active learning consists of big, splashy, group-oriented activities that are inappropriate for their course objectives, their teaching style, or their students' cognitive level. While we understand our colleagues' concerns, we do not accept these assumptions. We argue that all faculty can develop a repertoire of teaching strategies that are comfortable, meet course goals effectively, and engage students in the learning experience.

Faculty who have developed their own repertoires—through trial and error (and a little research) in their own classes—have written the chapters in this volume. We hope these chapters will appeal to all college and university faculty interested in alternative ways to achieve good teaching. The works in this volume are based on several assumptions: (1) active learning is necessary for student learning; (2) careful planning and structure are critical to the success of active learning; (3) the choice of strategies depends on course objectives, teaching style, and students' level of experience with content and activities; and (4) active learning approaches exist on a continuum from simple, short activities to complex, long activities.

The *active learning continuum* introduced in this volume is important given our concern that some faculty believe only complicated, group-oriented activities constitute genuine active learning. The continuum's framework underlines the importance of context in making decisions about teaching methods. Strong lecturers who make use of short, less complex strategies to enhance students' understanding and interest are practicing active learning just as legitimately as strong facilitators who organize entire classes with students in formal cooperative learning groups. This volume does not advocate active learning for its own sake, but rather the engagement of students in learning experiences that meet course goals and fit instructors' classroom styles. Whether strategies fall toward the simple or the complex end of the continuum, if students are effectively engaged, active learning is a success.

We have consciously provided a variety of perspectives in this volume by selecting authors from different types of institutions, different disciplines, and both genders, and those whose expertise falls on different parts of the active learning continuum. The chapters build a foundation for choosing and using active learning strategies; they provide specific examples and guidelines for several different approaches; and they explore issues that are emerging as these strategies gain wider acceptance. They are organized to reflect the continuum—the enhanced lecture at one end, with its shorter and simpler activities, and groupwork at the other end, with its more complex strategies.

1

The first chapter sets the stage for the rest of the volume by introducing the active learning continuum. Using our experience as faculty developers and teachers, we explore a framework that makes active learning methods accessible to all faculty. In Chapter Two, Judith E. Miller and associates James E. Groccia and John M. Wilkes use their research in the classroom to introduce the critical importance of structure in designing active learning approaches.

The next four chapters describe a variety of teaching approaches on the active learning continuum. Chapter Three illustrates how the periodic addition of short active learning activities can enhance students' learning in lecture-oriented classes. In Chapter Four, Eric H. Hobson explains the use of self-assessment activities to design writing assignments that encourage the development of cognitive and communication skills. In Chapter Five, David H. Gillette introduces ideas for using electronic tools to encourage student engagement in and out of the classroom. In Chapter Six, Karl A. Smith shows the benefits of cooperative learning strategies for designing effective group experiences. The final chapter examines issues that are emerging from growing interest in active learning. Together these chapters form a useful collection of ideas and methods for faculty who want to develop effective learning experiences.

In closing, we want to thank colleagues and friends for their contributions to this volume and to the development of our thinking about the engagement of students in learning. We are keenly aware that our reflections on the process of teaching and learning have developed over time, through interaction with others. Tracey particularly thanks Marylu McEwen for modeling the importance of reflecting on one's teaching, respecting students, and encouraging their involvement. Charles thanks Robin Higham, who first taught him the art of creating excitement in the classroom. We both owe particular thanks to Eric Hobson, Chris Gregory, and Tim Naegelin for thorough and humorous editing, and to Marilla Svinicki for her perceptive comments on our work in progress.

Tracey E. Sutherland
Charles C. Bonwell
Editors

TRACEY E. SUTHERLAND is director of faculty development at Truman State University (formerly Northeast Missouri State University), Kirksville, Missouri.

CHARLES C. BONWELL is professor of history and director of the Center for Teaching and Learning at the Saint Louis College of Pharmacy.

*We believe that all instructors should find ways to include
meaningful active learning approaches in their classes. This
chapter provides a framework for choosing active learning
strategies that take into account course objectives, teaching
styles, and students' level of experience.*

The Active Learning Continuum: Choosing Activities to Engage Students in the Classroom

Charles C. Bonwell, Tracey E. Sutherland

Our goal in this chapter is to develop a conceptual framework that allows all instructors to find ways to include meaningful active learning activities in their classes, regardless of their teaching style or course objectives. Although many ideas and suggestions are shared, this chapter is designed primarily to provoke reflection and discussion rather than to provide a definitive response to the issues involved.

Why Active Learning Strategies Are Needed

Teaching in the college classroom is becoming increasingly complicated. It is no longer sufficient for the college professor to be competent in a field of specialty and to "profess" a substantial base of knowledge to a classroom full of willing students. Today's effective college teachers must be prepared not only to share in-depth knowledge of their discipline but also to know something about college students and how they learn. Faculty are also expected to cultivate skills in different methods of teaching and assessment—areas in which they have had little or no preparation. Although these new expectations are unsettling for many instructors, the research evidence supporting active approaches as the more effective way to facilitate student learning cannot be ignored (Anderson and Adams, 1992; Chickering and Gamson, 1987; Johnson, Johnson, and Smith, 1991; McKeachie, Pintrich, Yi-Guang, and Smith, 1986). Students are simply more likely to internalize, understand, and remember material learned through active engagement in the learning process. Thus, the evidence clearly suggests the need for a change from the lecture that is so common in college classrooms (primarily teacher-talk), at the same time that college teachers are feeling uncertain of their preparation, experience, and skill in implementing the needed change.

Given these circumstances, it would be useful to have a framework that would allow faculty to consider their course objectives and teaching style and to determine through self-reflection what active learning strategies best meet their individual needs. For while developing teaching strategies that are less heavily based on the lecture method is certainly important, it is not the case that the lecture must be abandoned or that all faculty must begin using groupwork in their classes. What is important is for instructors to find approaches that fit their personal style of teaching and meet their educational objectives, while at the same time actively engaging students as they learn in the college classroom.

In our work with faculty we have many opportunities to discuss their concerns and the risks they perceive in beginning to incorporate active learning approaches into their classes. Bonwell and Eison (1991, pp. 59–64) note five of the commonly mentioned barriers to using active learning strategies: (1) one cannot cover as much content in class; (2) active learning requires too much time in preparation for class; (3) it seems impossible to use active learning approaches in large classes; (4) materials and resources are lacking; and (5) there are many risks to be considered, including how colleagues will perceive the legitimacy of the approaches, how student evaluations might be influenced, and how promotion and tenure might be affected.

These are valid concerns and not easily dismissed; it is understandable that faculty are reluctant to change their approaches to teaching. At the same time, the research indicating that students learn best when their intellectual engagement is high (a condition that is not likely to happen consistently in the traditional lecture-style class) is equally compelling. Integrating these two seemingly opposing perspectives is the focus of this chapter.

We are convinced by the research that all instructors should be using active learning strategies. We also believe that a wide variety of active learning strategies can be equally effective in the classroom. For instance, although numerous studies demonstrate that cooperative learning is superior to traditional lectures (Johnson, Johnson, and Smith, 1991), we are not aware of research-based studies that show formal cooperative learning to be superior to lectures that have been enhanced by interspersing a variety of active learning techniques. Thus, we do not assume that all faculty should be employing group teaching approaches, or any other particular methods, in their classes. Whether group-oriented strategies are appropriate for use in a given class would be determined by the instructor's course objectives and personal teaching style. Indeed, we are concerned that active learning is so often discussed in the context of groupwork that faculty who are not comfortable using group approaches or who feel that groupwork does not fit within their course objectives might believe that active learning approaches are not for them. The important consideration is student engagement in the learning process, and students can be strongly engaged and involved in learning without working in group settings.

A Conceptual Framework:
The Active Learning Continuum

For explicitly engaging students in the learning process we propose a conceptual framework focused on an active learning continuum that moves from simple tasks on one end to complex tasks on the other. We recognize that the use of a continuum—a line with two opposing characteristics, one at each endpoint—is an artificial, oversimplified construct, but we believe that it provides both a visual and conceptual model that is useful for designing courses that maximize students' intellectual engagement. Neither end of the continuum is considered to be "better" or "more desirable" than the other.

Consider an active learning continuum that looks like the following:

Simple tasks ───────────────────────────────── Complex tasks

For purposes of discussion, we define simple tasks as short and relatively unstructured, while complex tasks are of longer duration—perhaps the whole class period or longer—and are carefully planned and structured. Examples of endpoints on the active learning continuum might be a lecture punctuated by the pause procedure on one end and a cooperative learning class using the jigsaw procedure on the other.

The *pause procedure* (Ruhl and others, 1987) involves taking breaks at appropriate times in the lecture, every thirteen to eighteen minutes, to allow students to compare and rework their notes for two minutes. This technique has led to statistically significant increases in student learning on free recall quizzes at the end of the lecture and comprehensive examinations given twelve days later.

In a cooperative learning class, students work together in groups to meet course objectives. In the *jigsaw* strategy (Johnson, Johnson, and Smith, 1991), students participate in small subject-specific groups to learn a new concept, then return to home-base groups to teach the new concept to their fellow group members. Students working in their subject-specific groups not only learn the concept themselves but also ensure that other group members learn it, and that all members of the subject-specific group understand the new idea well enough to teach it to others when they return to their home-base groups. This strategy is described in detail in Chapter Six.

Tools for Choosing Activities That Explicitly
Engage Students

After teachers decide to include active learning strategies in a class, they must decide where those activities fit on the active learning continuum. The challenge is to choose approaches that meet the teachers' goals for students, fit their personal level of comfort with various teaching strategies, and furnish sufficient support for students so that active learning can be successful. Some tools are offered here to guide the selection of teaching approaches.

Course Objectives. When designing a course, perhaps the most important way to begin is to explicitly state what you and your students should accomplish in a given semester. One approach is to ask the following questions—a difficult, but necessary task:

What do I want my students to know (knowledge)? Although most of us would like for our students to take away from our classes as much knowledge as possible about our disciplines, studies show that there is a practical limit to how much students can learn in any given class period (Russell, Hendricson, and Herbert, 1984). This forces us to carefully examine the context of the course: Is it for majors or nonmajors? If for majors, what essential disciplinary concepts must they master at this level? If for nonmajors, what few concepts do I want students to remember about my discipline for the rest of their lives? Is this a course in a structured sequence? If so, am I aware of the content being presented and mastered in the other courses? What information can I reasonably expect students to acquire outside of the classroom? Answering these questions thoughtfully will help isolate precisely what knowledge students must acquire in the course.

What do I want students to be able to do (skills)? Although most faculty have a response to this question, those who focus primarily on content have not thought it their responsibility to teach skills explicitly. They presume that students will somehow acquire them on their own as they interact with the assigned material, write papers, solve problems, and give oral presentations. Over the years, however, as we hear reports of students who are adept at memorizing information but perform poorly in professional settings because they lack communication or problem solving skills, we have become convinced that as instructors we must explicitly teach students cognitive and professional skills, in addition to discipline content.

Acceptance of this proposition leads to another set of questions for course design: What skills are necessary to acquire and evaluate knowledge in my discipline? To what extent should students at this level be able to perform these skills? Under what circumstances can I teach these skills in or out of class? Are there general skills I can teach to support institutional objectives, such as locating and gathering information, critical thinking, communicating, understanding and articulating a value system, developing an aesthetic sense, and developing an appreciation for other cultures, past and present? The answers to these questions provide guidelines for developing active learning activities that are appropriate for students' needs.

In 1956, Benjamin Bloom and his colleagues published the *Taxonomy of Educational Objectives (Handbook 1: Cognitive Domain)*, a work that has had a significant impact on American education through its identification of levels of cognitive skills. In recent years, professors in higher education who are trying to explicitly teach thinking skills have found Bloom's taxonomy to be useful as a convenient structure for framing questions and developing exercises. Specifically, Bloom articulated six levels of thinking:

1. *Knowledge:* the ability to recall specific information, including facts, terminology, conventions, criteria, methodology, principles and theories.
2. *Comprehension:* the ability to understand the literal meaning of any communication. Bloom identified three types of comprehension behavior:
   a. *Translation:* taking what is being communicated and putting it into another form (different words, a graph, and so on)
   b. *Interpretation:* Reordering the ideas into a new configuration
   c. *Extrapolation:* Making estimates or predictions from a previous communication
3. *Application:* taking a principle or process previously learned and applying it in a new situation without being told to do so. Examples include applying social science generalizations to specific social problems or applying scientific or mathematical principles to practical situations.
4. *Analysis:* breaking material into its separate components, deducing their relationships, and understanding their pattern of organization. Examples include recognizing unstated assumptions, detecting cause and effect relationships, and recognizing forms and patterns in artistic works.
5. *Synthesis:* the creative process of putting parts or elements together into a new whole. This level includes writing a skillful essay, proposing ways to test hypotheses, and formulating theories that are applicable to social situations.
6. *Evaluation:* the process of making value judgments about ideas, solutions, methods, and so forth. These judgments can be quantitative or qualitative, but they must be based on the use of criteria or standards. Examples include evaluating the appropriateness of a health therapy or judging a work against standards in the discipline.

Although educational theorists may argue over certain aspects of this taxonomy, there is no doubt that it constitutes a practical framework for thinking about how we develop knowledge and skills in the classroom.

What do I want my students to feel (attitudes)? At first thought, many professors might recoil from an objective that smacks of something that seems less than rigorous, something not very academic. Upon reflection, however, most of us would probably admit that we would love our students to experience excitement as they discover the implications of our disciplinary material, or to feel the intellectual and emotional satisfaction that can come from solving a scientific problem or gaining insight into an historical issue. Couched in another way, at most institutions we visit, the lack of student motivation is a central concern of faculty. Fortunately, this seems to be an area in which the use of active learning can be helpful. McKeachie and colleagues (1986) found that active methods focusing on discussion motivated students more than straight lecture.

Indeed, for some disciplines the development of attitudes is an essential course goal. One of our colleagues, a nurse who teaches in a clinical setting, considers the development of compassion an important course objective for her students. Through role plays and simulations, she places her students in situations designed to foster empathy and understanding for those who are seriously ill. Similarly, the proliferation of business ethics courses at colleges and universities across the country suggests that attitudes are an important component in that discipline as well.

When trying to decide what relative weight to give to knowledge, skills, and attitudes, the following diagram may prove helpful:

Continuum of Course Objectives

Acquisition of knowledge ———————————— Acquisition of skills/attitudes

A number of factors determine where a course and its objectives might fall on this continuum. An introductory science course required of majors might be heavily weighted toward the knowledge endpoint, focusing on conceptual and factual material that must be mastered prior to taking the next course in a departmental sequence. In an introductory course for nonmajors, however, the mix might be quite different. An instructor might decide that if this might be the last chemistry course some students ever take she would prefer to emphasize the solution of interesting and relevant problems, in order to better motivate students through an understanding of how the power of chemistry and the scientific method can affect their daily lives. This kind of course might include a number of activities designed to promote the development of skills and attitudes, and it might place less emphasis on the acquisition of knowledge. Both approaches are appropriate depending on the context of the class. (For a more extensive description of how to design a course, see Lovell-Troy and Eickmann, 1992).

Personal Style. We believe that it is necessary for each of us to reflect on our teaching style and its implications for our choices of active learning techniques. Instructors' personal styles are a deciding factor in determining the level of interaction they can be comfortable with in the classroom. For our purposes, *interaction* refers to the level of interplay between an instructor and students and the level of interplay between students and other students. The concept can be can be represented as follows:

Interaction in a Classroom

Limited interaction ———————————————— Extensive interaction

Where on this continuum instructors prefer their classrooms to be depends on several factors, including the instructors' personality characteristics, preference for particular teaching methods, comfort with levels of control, willingness to take risks, and perception of their role in the classroom.

Personality Characteristics. There are a variety of frameworks that might be used to describe characteristics of personality. Theories and instruments abound from the literature in psychology, business, education, political science, and other fields. As an example we will use the conceptual model of the Myers-Briggs Type Indicator (MBTI) to explore how personal style affects an instructor's comfort level with interaction in the classroom.

The MBTI is based on psychologist Carl Jung's theory of psychological "types" (Myers and Myers, 1980), which provides a model that explains why people take in information (perception) and make decisions (judgment) differently. *Four functions* describe different approaches to perception and judgment. The perceptive processes are *sensing* (S) and *intuition* (N). People who most prefer sensing take in information primarily through the five senses, while those who prefer intuition perceive possibilities, meanings, and relationships by way of insight. The two kinds of *judgment* use the terms *thinking* (T) and *feeling* (F) in a specific way to describe two rational processes used for decision making. Those who prefer thinking use principles of cause and effect to decide issues, and tend to be impersonal in their approach. Feeling types, however, decide by considering the values and merits of the issues involved, and tend to consider how others will be affected by decisions.

The Jungian framework also includes *four attitudes* that guide how people interact with the outer world. *Extraversion* (E) and *introversion* (I) describe the direction of a person's energy flow. An extravert's attention and energy flow out toward the environment, while an introvert's energy is focused inward toward the world of thoughts and ideas. The other two attitudes, *judging* (J) and *perceiving* (P), describe preferences for a style of living. People who prefer judging seek organization, closure, decision making, and planning in their lifestyle, while perceiving types prefer flexibility, seeing all sides of issues, and staying open to new events.

The MBTI combines the four mental processes and the four attitudes, E or I, S or N, T or F, and J or P to make sixteen possible types, which are represented by the combination of letters, for example, ENFJ or INTP. It is important to note that while anyone taking the MBTI will end up with a four-letter type describing their preferences for certain ways of doing things, the theory assumes that everyone can use all four functions and all four attitudes. A person's type indicates his or her *preference* for one function or attitude over the others. (For more detailed information on the Myers-Briggs Type Indicator, see Myers and McCaulley, 1985, and Myers and Myers, 1980.)

Using this framework, it is easy to think of times when personality style might affect a teacher's choice of active learning strategies. A professor who is very extraverted (E) will be more comfortable choosing activities with lots of interaction, while an introvert (I) may be reluctant to design an approach that forces him to constantly focus energy out into the class, leaving little time for reflection and careful consideration. A teacher who prefers judging (J) will insist on organization and control when choosing group strategies, while a more perceiving (P) instructor will enjoy giving students more control within a flexible design. No single type is better at teaching or using active learning strategies. It is choosing strategies that fit our personal style that makes the difference.

Levels of Control. In our experience, the issue of control is one of the least discussed dimensions of classroom teaching. Faculty, particularly those who prefer a high degree of control over what occurs in the classroom, hesitate to admit to a characteristic that popular literature presents as something less than desirable. Experience suggests, however, that control is an important element in determining how comfortable a teacher will be with different active learning strategies. Many teachers are not at ease with a high degree of spontaneity in the classroom or with wide-ranging, unstructured discussions that rapidly leap from one topic to another. For them, structured activities focused on specific topics for allocated periods of time will be more appropriate. Others for whom control is less an issue may be comfortable with any unstructured activity, including collaborative learning, in which students set the agenda, devise activities necessary to achieve their goals, and create assessment tools to see whether they have been successful.

We should think reflectively about our classroom practice, for we may not be aware to what degree control is an issue. For instance, a colleague who teaches a demanding anatomy and physiology course that is feared by many students agreed to try the pause procedure in his lectures. When asked about it later, he focused on two students sitting at the back of the class who did not compare notes when asked to do so. "Did they bother anyone?" "No." "So what is the issue?" Pause. "It's about control, isn't it?" This instructor persisted and later became comfortable with the pause procedure and other short activities. Indeed, the power of his introduction of these techniques is illustrated by a comment from a business major who talked about taking the same anatomy course for *fun* during a later semester: "You know, Dr. _____ is so laid back that he stops and lets us compares notes or ask questions about what he is presenting. He really cares about us learning the material!"

Preference for Teaching Methods. Our preference for certain teaching methods often develops through a process of acculturation. Most of us have come through systems where the professor lectured and the teaching assistants led discussions. Not surprisingly, after receiving our doctorates we adopted the method of our mentors. Others, without any training in how to lead discussions and lacking support for problems, found the experience as a teaching assistant excruciating. Not surprisingly they now choose to lecture. Further, there are disciplinary expectations that can create conformity, particularly for junior faculty. Departments in which teaching is done in a given fashion expect others to teach accordingly. All of this suggests, given our cultural traditions, that it is unrealistic to expect that all of us will—or should—dramatically change the way we teach. (Fortunately, as we learned earlier in this chapter from our colleague in the anatomy and physiology course, even small changes systematically implemented over time can have a significant impact in our classrooms.)

The Effect of Risk. As we talk to faculty around the country about adopting active learning, the fear of failure is often a pervasive theme in our discussions. Many faculty acknowledge that they have little understanding of what active learning is or how to implement it in their classrooms. As a result, they understandably resist others' efforts to convince them to change their teaching methods. To address these concerns, Bonwell and Eison (1991) developed a model designed to minimize perceived risk. They suggest that faculty can lessen the risks associated with active learning by controlling the amount of time devoted to the task (shorter activities have less risk), by planning the activity carefully, and by providing sufficient structure to keep students on task.

Perception of Role. Our perceived role in the classroom is an important determinant in choosing the types of activities we will be comfortable using. Numerous workshops have shown us that most faculty see their principle role as providing students with the information necessary to understand the discipline. Indeed, this perception, coupled with the exponential growth of knowledge in our disciplines, often leads faculty to assume that there is no time left for active learning activities concentrated on other educational objectives. Some faculty, formerly constrained in a similar fashion, have learned to separate out that which must be taught in the class and that which can assigned to students as their responsibility to learn outside of the classroom. This process can be made explicit with study guides detailing the factual information (Bloom's *knowledge* level) that students must acquire on their own. This allows class time to be used more efficiently to help students understand material that past experience has shown the instructor is more difficult for students to understand (usually at higher levels of Bloom's taxonomy). Chapter Three illustrates how active learning activities can support those efforts.

Student Experience. Another element to be considered by instructors prior to selecting active learning strategies is the level of student experience. We believe it is important to determine at the outset how much experience students have with different active learning strategies, and to what extent they have mastered requisite disciplinary skills. The answers to these questions determine how much structure and how much support the students will require as the course progresses. The instructor's perception of students' experience can be charted on the following continuum:

Levels of Student Experience

Inexperienced ————————————————————————— Experienced

Depending on the nature of any given class, students may be either inexperienced or quite experienced with both the content and nontraditional teaching approaches. Upper-division students in courses in their major are likely to have experience with both disciplinary skills and the teaching strategies typically used within their discipline. Students in lower-division and general education courses may be more inexperienced, in both content and teaching strategies.

In large part the success of active learning techniques depends on a classroom environment that allows students to feel comfortable taking risks and provides sufficient structure to meet students' needs. These elements are particularly important when using an approach with students who are inexperienced in either the material, the method, or both. An instructor's best intentions to conduct a discussion in class can falter when students do not respond because they are too nervous or unsure of what the professor is looking for. Without adequate structure for the activity and a safe environment, inexperienced students will be reluctant to participate. If an activity is new to a majority of the class, it must be carefully structured and repeated until students become comfortable.

Using These Tools. The continuums presented in this chapter are intended to provide a framework that faculty can use to choose active learning strategies that are both comfortable and effective for achieving their course goals. With some preparation and a bit of courage, everyone can develop a collection of approaches that will be successful in their classes.

A faculty member can use the continuums of course objectives, interaction in the classroom, and level of student experience as tools to indicate where their preferences for course design might fall on the active learning continuum. For example, if a course's objectives focus primarily on students attaining knowledge, the students in the course are fairly inexperienced with the material, and the teacher's style is to prefer more control and less interaction in the class, then the faculty member might choose active learning activities that fall more toward the "simple tasks" end of the active learning continuum. However, if a teacher's objectives for a course are the development of clinical skills, the students are seniors and well-versed in the material, and the teacher is comfortable with a high level of classroom interaction and spontaneous activity, then the instructor might choose activities closer to the "complex tasks" end of the active learning continuum. These examples are broad generalizations, but they are presented here to demonstrate how these continuums can be used to consider the kinds of active learning activities that are appropriate for a particular course and instructor.

Examples from Practice

The continuum framework is intended to provide questions that will stimulate faculty to consider the kinds of active learning approaches that will fit their course objectives, teaching preferences, and students' level of experience. First, what is the focus of the course objectives? Next, what level of interaction in the classroom is comfortable for the instructor? Then, what is the level of students' experience? And finally, what kind of active learning activities best fit the answers to the above questions? The examples that follow illustrate a couple of approaches to using this framework for choosing active learning strategies.

A Case in Literature. A professor of English decided to change his world literature course to place more focus on students gaining an appreciation of the cultural contexts of the literature they studied. He was an experienced instructor and enjoyed brief discussions during class lectures. He felt ready to explore using additional approaches. His literature course was a general education requirement, likely to be made up of students from various majors with little previous exposure to the content. Considering his course objectives, teaching style, and the level of his students' experience, he designed the course around a series of lectures supplemented with short, well-structured group presentations.

Using the Continuum of Course Objectives. The course would fall primarily toward the "knowledge" end of the course objective continuum. Emphasis would be placed on understanding the literature and its cultural context rather than on acquiring skills or attitudes.

Using the Continuum of Interaction in the Classroom. The teacher considered his style to be relaxed and reflective. He felt comfortable with some class discussion but preferred to control the direction of conversation to be certain that course content was covered—toward the middle of the interaction continuum.

Considering the Continuum of Level of Student Experience. The class would be made up of students from a mix of majors and ranging from first-year students to juniors, so the teacher knew that most of them would be relatively unfamiliar with the course content, near the inexperienced end of the student experience continuum.

Choosing an Appropriate Place on the Active Learning Continuum. The professor of English decided that his course objectives and teaching style put him toward the middle of the active learning continuum but closer to the "simple tasks" end. His course content was pretty firmly in the area of acquiring knowledge. He was comfortable with classroom interaction when it was limited and controlled, and he knew that his students' level of experience would be limited. Considering the continuum, he decided to use active learning strategies that were simple, short, and relatively unstructured. He developed a combination lecture/presentation format that involved students in group projects but kept classroom interaction at a very controlled and predictable level.

Given his comfort with a more controlled class setting and his success using interactive lectures, he decided to begin each class with a thirty-minute lecture addressing background material on the topic of the day. Group presentations by students, including slides of cultural and artistic artifacts, would make up the next fifteen minutes. Given his students' relative inexperience, he planned to carefully structure this assignment. The course design was deliberately repetitive, to allow inexperienced students to become comfortable in a more active classroom environment, and because he knew he would be more comfortable with a simple class format. Using groups to make presentations was a stretch for him, so he planned for their presentations to be short.

Since his course objectives centered primarily on cultivating knowledge, the instructor developed an activity he dubbed "model note taking." During each group presentation, a member from another group was assigned to take notes using an overhead projector at the front of the class. At the end of the class, after the discussion of the groups' presentations, the model notetaker reviewed the notes with the class. The transparencies were a permanent record of class discussions and could be used later for test reviews (Leavens, 1992). The professor thought this simple approach would bring a new dimension to the class, helping students to focus on the most important elements of the new material they were learning.

A Case in Nursing. Although her course in community health nursing was, by its nature, participation oriented, the professor of nursing wanted to get students more involved in its classroom component. The fieldwork for the course provided hands-on experience, allowing upper-division students to further hone their skills in patient care. Changes in the classroom section would support learning teamwork skills as well as content. The professor decided that her students' maturity and experience and the nature of her course objectives would allow for variety in teaching approaches. She had a strong background in using active strategies both at the college level and in community education settings. With these things in mind, she decided to expand the active learning elements in the classroom component of the course.

Using the Continuum of Course Objectives. The objectives for the course included both strengthening content areas and developing collaborative skills. In the professor's view, work settings for professional nurses would require them to excel at teamwork. She designed the course to heavily emphasize the development of team skills and interdependent attitudes.

Considering the Continuum of Interaction in the Classroom. The instructor considered herself to be the consummate extrovert (it was her strongest score on the Myers-Briggs Type Indicator). She enjoyed her classes most when everyone participated and when students held responsibility for much of what happened during any meeting of the class.

Using the Continuum of Level of Student Experience. The students in the class were older than traditional college-age students, and experienced, both in the content and with more participative methods. The professor knew they would be able to handle a variety of active learning approaches.

Choosing an Appropriate Place on the Active Learning Continuum. Given her course objectives, personal style, and experienced students, the nursing professor placed herself near the "complex tasks" end of the active learning continuum. While definitely focused on content, her course would emphasize development of skills in teamwork and attitudes of interdependence. She was quite comfortable with considerable unstructured classroom interaction, and her students were well-prepared in course content and experienced in participative learning environments. Considering the continuum, she planned to use highly interactive group activities, occasionally interspersed with mini-lectures by the instructor. She structured group activities to meet course objectives, then let students do the planning while she circulated to serve as a facilitator and resource when needed.

Major content areas were divided among groups of three to four students, each group having complete responsibility for teaching their area—from developing objectives to developing tests. One of the objectives of the course was to practice teamwork skills, so the instructor planned to devote most of the first two classes to discussing group dynamics and practicing effective collaborative strategies. The class would develop rules for groupwork that addressed shared responsibility, organizational structures, and appropriate expectations. The professor planned to meet regularly with the groups, to monitor their progress and ensure that important points would be addressed in their presentations to the class. Each major content area would be covered in very different ways, but as strolling facilitator and group consultant the professor could ensure that her course goals were realized.

Summary

The evidence that active learning approaches are an effective way to facilitate learning is too compelling to ignore. While we understand the barriers that discourage faculty from considering use of these approaches, we believe that with consideration of course objectives, teaching styles, and students' level of experience it is possible for all faculty to find active learning strategies that can work for them. The continuum framework presented in this chapter is intended to guide instructors through a series of questions that will help them define the kinds of alternatives that will be both comfortable and enjoyable, and that will support students' learning.

References

Anderson, J. A., and Adams, M. "Acknowledging the Learning Styles of Diverse Student Populations: Implications for Instructional Design." In L.L.B. Border and N.V.N. Chism (eds.), *Teaching for Diversity*. New Directions for Teaching and Learning, no. 49. San Francisco: Jossey-Bass, 1992.

Bloom, B. S. (ed.). *Taxonomy of Educational Objectives: The Classification of Educational Goals.* New York: Longman, 1956.

Bonwell, C. C., and Eison, J. A. *Active Learning: Creating Excitement in the Classroom.* ASHE-ERIC Higher Education Report No. 1. Washington, D.C.: School of Education and Human Development, George Washington University, 1991.

Chickering, A. W., and Gamson, Z. F. "Seven Principles for Good Practice." *AAHE Bulletin,* 1987, *39,* 3–7.

Johnson, D. W., Johnson, R. T., and Smith, K. A. *Cooperative Learning: Increasing College Faculty Instructional Productivity.* ASHE-ERIC Higher Education Report No. 4. Washington, D.C.: School of Education and Human Development, George Washington University, 1991.

Leavens, D. *Cultural Contexts in World Literature.* Jepson Fellowship Project Proposal. Kirksville: Northeast Missouri State University, 1992.

Lovell-Troy, L., and Eickmann, P. *Course Design for College Teachers.* Englewood Cliffs, N.J.: Educational Technology Publications, 1992.

McKeachie, W. J., Pintrich, P. R., Yi-Guang, L., and Smith, D.A.F. *Teaching and Learning in the College Classroom: A Review of the Research Literature.* Ann Arbor: Regents of the University of Michigan, 1986.

Myers, I. B., and McCaulley, M. H. *Manual: A Guide to the Development and Use of the Myers-Briggs Type Indicator.* Palo Alto: Consulting Psychologists Press, 1985.

Myers, I. B., and Myers, P. B. *Gifts Differing.* Palo Alto: Consulting Psychologists Press, 1980.

Ruhl, K. L., Hughes, C. A., and Schloss, P. J. "Using the Pause Procedure to Enhance Lecture Recall." *Teacher Education and Special Education,* 1987, *10,* 14–18.

Russell, I. J., Hendricson, W. D., and Herbert, R. J. "Effects of Lecture Information Density on Medical Student Achievement." *Journal of Medical Education,* 1984, *59,* 881–889.

CHARLES C. BONWELL is professor of history and director of the Center for Teaching and Learning at the Saint Louis College of Pharmacy.

TRACEY E. SUTHERLAND is director of faculty development at Truman State University (formerly Northeast Missouri State University), Kirksville, Missouri.

This chapter describes the various ways that the level and type of structure can be varied in an active learning course and discusses how to use the manipulation of course structure to meet the challenges presented by a diverse student body.

Providing Structure:
The Critical Element

Judith E. Miller, James E. Groccia, John M. Wilkes

Issues of structure do not arise in courses taught in the traditional lecture format. The teacher typically retains complete control of content, pacing, evaluation, and procedures. Such courses are usually highly structured, and by virtue of their many years of experience with the format students know exactly what to expect. When varying amounts of authority and responsibility for learning are handed over to students, however, the challenge of learning both new material and new ways of learning must be balanced by the support of adequate structure, in the form of clearly defined tasks, guidance through the (sometimes traumatic) process of groupwork with peers, milestones, feedback, and reassurance that the nature of knowledge is that it is not always possible to know the right answer. Paradoxically, it is precisely in these areas that many teachers fall short. Today's teachers were the students who performed well in, and may have been most comfortable with, the traditional lecture format. Consequently, they are masters of the high-structure, low-student-involvement classroom environment, and they are less comfortable navigating in, much less creating, environments in which teacher control is relinquished. A common mistake of teachers in first adopting an active learning strategy is to relinquish structure along with control, and the common result is for students to feel frustrated and disoriented. Actually, course design, up-front organization, and integrated transitions are more demanding and crucial in an active learning course in which indirect influence, rather than minute-to-minute control, remains entirely within the teacher's authority.

Researchers (Cronbach and Snow, 1977; Glaser, 1968; Miller, Wilkes, and Cheetham, 1993) have noted that no single teaching approach or course structure is optimal for all students. Student diversity in terms of cognitive style, personality, individual preferences for teaching style, achievement, motivation, and other variables suggests that attention to structure and its influence on learning and student satisfaction is critical to successful implementation of teaching strategies. In this chapter we focus on the challenge created by such a diversity of needs.

What the Literature Says About Structure and Cognitive Development

In a general sense, structure can be defined as the way parts are arranged or put together to form a whole, the interrelation of parts, or the principle of organization in a complex entity (The American Heritage Dictionary, 1985). In an educational setting, structure incorporates all of these meanings, describing how, and how much, the course experience is determined by the teacher.

Structure. The interaction between student characteristics and course structure in traditional learning environments has received much attention over the years. The degree and type of structure in an instructional situation interacts with student characteristics to affect achievement (Cronbach, 1957; Cronbach and Snow, 1977; Domino, 1971; Shaw, 1975; Smith, Wood, Downer, and Raygor, 1956). In one study (Blizek, Jackson, and LaVoie, 1974), highly motivated students performed better in and were more favorably disposed toward a short-course independent study format, and conversely, poorly motivated students performed better in a conventional lecture/discussion course structure. The authors concluded that one course structure may not be suitable for all students at all times. The literature indicates that task structure is usually under the instructor's direct control and is a variable that directly impacts student learning (Pilkonis, 1977; Daly and Buss, 1984; Booth-Butterfield, 1986).

Cognitive Development. College students traverse a series of stages of cognitive development in which their thinking becomes more complex. One researcher, William Perry (1970), developed a framework for understanding students' intellectual and moral development that comprises ten positions. Perry describes students moving through stages, from "dualistic thinking" at the lowest point through "multiplicity" at the midpoint to a "commitment in relativism" at the highest point. A more familiar scheme is Bloom's taxonomy of educational objectives (Bloom, 1956; Gronlund and Linn, 1990), which categorizes cognitive tasks, in ascending order of complexity, as knowledge, comprehension, application, analysis, synthesis, and evaluation (for a detailed description of these categories, see Chapter One). For teachers using active learning, the implication of Perry's scheme and Bloom's taxonomy is that beginning students require more structure (in terms of defined course content and explicit task design) than more advanced students. Although progress from one of Perry's positions to another is measured in terms of months, and could seldom be expected to result from experiences in a single course, the authors have had success with sequencing tasks through a course, and even within an individual assignment, such that the tasks begin at the lower levels of cognitive functioning (reiteration of known facts—Bloom's level of "knowledge") and progress to higher levels (evaluation of arguments—Bloom's level of "evaluation") (Bloom, 1956). An example is given later.

Cognitive Styles. Theories of cognitive development lead to the conclusion that the appropriate progression of tasks is from structured to less structured. However, this strategy works only up to a point. Within the diversity of any classroom some students are more comfortable with less structured and some with more structured tasks. It is not so clear that, given the cognitive mix in any group of students, all students are best served if less structured tasks are held until last. Claxton and Murrill (1987) are a good source of further information on cognitive styles.

Our studies have been informed by a cognitive style typology based on the cognitive dimensions of *differentiation* (Gordon and Morse, 1969) and *remote association* (Mednick, 1963). Differentiation is a critical evaluative ability that focuses on problem identification and formulation. Remote association is a flexible method of problem solving involving rapid, nonlogical, intuitive approaches. We use a fifteen-minute paper-and-pencil measure that identifies students as either "Problem Solvers" who excel at remote association; "Problem Finders," who are adept at differentiation; "Integrators," who are strong in both approaches; and "Implementors," who have low scores on both cognitive dimensions, although they certainly do not have low intelligence. Students in different majors have been found to have different cognitive style distributions, but it is safe to assume that all four cognitive types will be represented in any class.

Our study confirmed the hypothesis that students' reactions to an active learning introductory biology course varies depending on the degree of structure of course tasks and the students' cognitive styles. Problem Solvers tended to excel in tasks where the problem was well-defined but the solution was open-ended, while Problem Finders preferred tasks where the problem was ill-defined. Implementors favored highly structured tasks that could be completed by persistent effort and logical extrapolation without intuitive leaps. The Integrators proved to be adaptable under most circumstances, flourishing when faced with the dual challenge of mastering complicated underlying materials in order to address open-ended problems that in turn needed to be developed and specified. Their adaptability made the Integrators most able to use the more complex kinds of thinking described by both Bloom's taxonomy and Perry's scheme. Our study suggests that a progression from more structure early in a course to less structure later on is not ideal for all students.

Planning Strategies for Course Structure

Course objectives should be the basis for the design of structure for all courses. The context of the course must also be taken into account. Students' levels of experience, class size, and whether students will be majors or nonmajors all affect how a course should be structured for greatest effectiveness.

Course Objectives. No course revision should be undertaken without careful review, and perhaps revision, of course and curriculum objectives. If objectives drive both task design and evaluation, then evaluations of student progress will test what you teach, and that always makes for happier students. It is essential that course objectives be communicated to students in writing at the beginning of the course.

Many but not all objectives will probably relate to course content. Introductory courses may emphasize lower levels of Bloom's taxonomy, whereas advanced courses may include more analysis, synthesis, and evaluation in their list of objectives. Some course objectives, especially in active learning courses, can and probably should relate to personal development (appreciation of differences in background, ethnicity, work styles, and personality, and the eradication of stereotypes) and professional skills (oral and written communication, teamwork, and problem solving).

Clearly, course objectives and course structure must be congruent. If the development of teamwork skills is not an important course objective, or if its importance is not clearly communicated, students will be less likely to gracefully accept a course structure that requires them to work in teams. Similarly, it is essential that active learning activities—be they breaks in an enhanced lecture or out-of-class group projects—have as their subject matter the central concepts and objectives of the course. For example, one of this chapter's authors, Miller, chooses project topics to motivate the study of basic biological concepts. In one term, the theme was whether Vietnam veterans should be compensated for the health effects of Agent Orange exposure. After some initial reading, students identified cancer, birth defects, and neurological damage as relevant topics. In turn, the study of cancer motivated the study of cell division and regulation of gene expression.

Fitting the Structure to the Context. Both the amount of structure and its details will vary in different course contexts. As a rule, first-year students and those who are beginning in a discipline require more structure than students who are older, intellectually advanced, and experienced in the discipline. Such structure may take the form of more lecture time, more quizzes and other forms of interim feedback, more explicit and fewer open-ended tasks, and more face-to-face support from course staff when doing long-term out-of-class projects. Advanced students, particularly those experienced in active learning, can comfortably handle even open-ended laboratory research projects if some structure is provided in the form of weekly meetings with course staff, either in the lab or outside of class, and regular class meetings. Students majoring in the discipline are far more likely to be willing to consider the open questions in the discipline, whereas nonmajors tend to want "just the facts." In effect, regardless of their level of intellectual maturity, nonmajors seem to operate at a lower level in a discipline that is not their own.

Class size and available staff resources are important considerations in structuring an active learning course. In our experience, in a small class (up to about thirty students) a single instructor can handle the logistics of almost any active learning activity. In larger classes, active learning activities must be carefully planned with an eye to logistics. The major drain on an instructor's time in an active learning class is office traffic, which becomes unmanageable and all-consuming in larger classes. Therefore, if additional staff are not available to assist individual students or groups with out-of-class projects, or if student meetings outside of class are difficult to arrange (for example with commuting students), then more activities must be done during class time, and they must then be less time-consuming and require less outside research. That does not mean, however, that the tasks need to be either less challenging or less important.

The content of the course also determines structure to some extent. We argue strongly that even students in introductory-level courses should be exposed to some of the uncertainties and emerging issues in the discipline. However, an elementary Spanish course will of necessity contain more structured content than a course in cross-cultural psychology. In this context, "structured content" refers to a prevailing field consensus; but even structured content can be conveyed to students through active involvement (for example, through conversation or writing about topics of their choosing).

Finally, the instructor's own level of comfort is a crucial factor in determining the level and type of structure in active learning classes. We echo Bonwell and Eison (1991) in their suggestion that it is all right to start small: it is not necessary to abandon lecturing completely, nor is it necessary (or desirable) to restructure the course in one fell swoop. We also second Felder (1995) in pointing out that it is all right to try something new and fail. Not everything that we try will work for us, or in our specific context, and it takes time to arrive at a style that fits. The important thing is to reflect on experience, learn from mistakes, and try again. That is the behavior we want to model for our students, isn't it?

The Levels of Structure

When considering the structure of a course, it is important to plan for preparing students for a new kind of format, for making the flow of content and activities clear and purposeful, for using the time formerly consumed by lecture in ways that work toward course objectives, and for using grading mechanisms that students perceive as fairly measuring course goals.

Structuring the Intellectual Environment. Planning for structure should occur at all levels of a course for an optimum course experience. First, it is helpful to structure the intellectual environment for the students by cultivating the mindset that this course will be different. This is a wonderful opportunity to create excitement for the upcoming adventure of shared inquiry and active intellectual involvement rather than to describe the environment in terms of procedures and requirements. This can be done by carefully crafting an introductory statement or activity that communicates both the course objectives and the teacher's openness and enthusiasm. Since objectives in an active learning course presumably involve more than just mastery of a body of information, the affective objectives, which may be unfamiliar to students, may require some explanation. Miller has had success with an introductory exercise in which she asks students to work in pairs to construct a list of the skills their first employer will be looking for. She then writes the list, which is invariably heavy on items such as "ability to work in teams," "written and oral communication skills," "problem solving ability," and "ability to learn on my own," on the blackboard. Then, as she checks off certain items she points out that a traditional lecture course addresses only one item on the list—"mastery of subject area"—whereas this active learning course will work on several of those items.

Structuring the Curriculum Flow and Tasks. As we have discussed in the context of Perry's scheme and Bloom's taxonomy, curriculum flow must also be structured. It is especially important for younger students or those less experienced in independent project work and teamwork that early assignments be highly structured—that is, the sequence of tasks the students must perform should be clearly laid out in a step-by-step fashion, with the less structured tasks reserved for later in the course.

For example, in an early project Miller asks the students to design a biological membrane made of protein (rather than the usual lipid). She begins by asking students to review the structure and biological properties of lipids, proteins, and biological membranes, and bases a homework assignment and discussion section meeting on that task. Students are then asked to figure out how to assemble proteins into a membrane that would function similarly to a lipid membrane, a task that is open-ended (there is no single right answer) but still fairly highly structured (the task to be done is clearly laid out). This task is in contrast to a highly unstructured project assigned much later in the course, in which students are asked to identify the underlying causes of an environmental problem of their own choosing, suggest a solution, and write a research proposal evaluating their recommended approach. Note that even though one of these sample tasks is highly structured and one is highly unstructured, within each task there is a progression of subtasks from structured and fact-based to unstructured and open-ended.

The complexity of the underlying material that must be mastered in order for students to accomplish each task also deserves consideration. Although it may not always be possible to progress from least-complex to most-complex material, the challenge of complex underlying material should be balanced with extra support in the form of frequent feedback and a more structured task.

Finally, it is important to take into account the cognitive diversity within a class. Teachers usually, and inadvertently, teach to the cognitive style that matches their own. During the course, tasks should be assigned that allow students of different cognitive styles to shine. With respect to the cognitive style typology we have described, this means that some tasks should require students to explain an ill-defined problem (for example, the assignment cited above in which students were asked to identify the underlying causes of an environmental problem) and some should require them to use creativity to arrive at an open-ended solution to a well-defined problem (for example, designing a membrane made out of proteins). At times these alternatives can be provided by giving students choices of questions to answer. However, a balance must be struck between allowing all students to shine at least some of the time and "stretching" students in directions that may be unfamiliar and uncomfortable, for the sake of developing new skills. It therefore makes sense to have course content consist of a mixture of tasks requiring different cognitive skills so that all students must grapple with all the stages of creativity at least some of the time.

Structuring the Class Meetings. A dilemma for teachers using active learning is how to use time formerly filled by lectures. Certainly there is still a place for lecture in the active learning course because some material would be very difficult for students to assemble and synthesize for themselves, particularly if a variety of learning resources are used. Lecture time can also be used for large-group discussions, quizzes, and short individual and small-group cooperative activities (for example, critical thinking questions, concept maps, or one-minute papers) timed to provide a break from the lecture every fifteen to twenty minutes. A lecture need not reiterate material in the textbook, but it can be structured to provide an overview of the materials (for example, from the original scientific literature) that students are encountering in the current unit or project.

Conference periods, which can be run by teaching assistants, provide rich opportunities for student involvement. These sessions are regular class periods set aside for conferences. They should be carefully designed, by collaboration between the professor and the teaching assistants, to have defined objectives and a clearly structured path by which those objectives will be achieved. For example, students can be assigned individual written homework, due in conference. Thus prepared, they can confer in teams in class to arrive at a consensus answer on a portion of the homework and present it to the class in some way. Teaching assistants or the instructor may then introduce new material (sometimes a videotape or a game simulation) for analysis by the students in the light of their answers to the homework. This is also an excellent time for individual or small-group oral reports on out-of-class projects.

Structuring the Assessment Process. In designing assessments, it is vital to revisit course objectives. For example, Miller tells students that learning to solve scientific problems, to work in teams, to communicate orally and in writing, and to find information independently are the most important course objectives. Consequently, 60 percent or more of the final course grade is based on group-produced oral and written reports, and less than 15 percent is based on closed-book quizzes.

In teaching an active learning course, if you expect students to share ideas or information in class or in individual discussion, it is essential that the grading scheme not foster competition. When grades are curved, or "norm-referenced," students who do well do so only if others do poorly. Therefore, it is to a student's advantage to prevent classmates from obtaining valuable information, and even more advantageous to sabotage their efforts. Active learning that involves interpersonal interaction is much more successful when grading is "criterion-referenced," comparing all students with a standard of performance. In that case, all students could, in theory, earn A's. Cooperation, since it results in better work, also results in more learning and higher grades for all students.

Groupwork always presents the dilemma of how much of the grade to assign for individual assignments and tests and how much to assign on the basis of group products. The particular combination of individual and group assessment is a matter of personal preference and philosophy, and it varies among teachers and courses, as does the more controversial decision of how much grading should be done by peers. In Miller's course, some assignments receive group grades assigned by the professor (for example, the written project reports), some receive group grades assigned by the other students in the course (for example, the oral project reports), some receive individual grades assigned by the course staff (for example, the quizzes and homework), and some receive individual grades assigned by peers (written project report grades are modified by a peer-determined "multiplier" that gives group members the chance to evaluate each other's contributions). The peer-graded oral reports are noncontroversial and seem to promote attendance at the oral report sessions. The peer-determined multiplier is quite controversial in groups in which dynamics or division of labor are issues, but nevertheless it puts some real teeth into the course objective on teamwork, and therefore has a positive effect on intragroup communication.

An Example from Practice

Miller has taught a two-course introductory sequence in general biology in an active (and cooperative) learning format since 1989. She and her colleagues have collected a longitudinal data set and conducted extensive analyses concerning the relationships among student satisfaction, performance, cognitive style, group dynamics, and task type. The results are summarized here because they illustrate both mistakes made through an ignorance of elements of structure, and successes that resulted when the effects of various levels of structure were finally understood.

The course was developed by Miller and Cheetham (1990), out of ignorance and unbridled idealism, as a highly unstructured course in which lectures and tests were totally abandoned in favor of in-class group discussion and out-of-class groupwork. As a term-long project, students were asked to develop a closed life-support system for long-term space flight. Class discussions and library resources provided (far from adequate) support. Students were disoriented and overwhelmed by the lack of structure and the magnitude of the tasks, and demanded more of the trappings of the traditional course. Interpretation of the students' comments in light of the authors' experience suggests that they needed the structure of more guidance through the tasks, regular feedback on their progress, and reassurance (in the form of quizzes) that they were really learning some biology. During the next several course offerings, structure was reintroduced in the form of limited lecturing and quizzes. We became more modest in our expectations of first-year students' capacity for independent problem solving, and thus introduced more structure and more feedback into the tasks we assigned. In addition, we learned to prevent at least some problems of group dynamics by increasing the impact of peer evaluations (within the small working group) on each student's course grade and by forming groups based on scheduling preferences for out-of-class meeting times.

As a result of these modifications in various aspects of course structure, overall student satisfaction improved. However, although average satisfaction was about the same as it had been in the traditional lecture course, we continued to be mystified by the polarity of student opinion, ranging from "This course was worth the entire $20,000 I spent to come to WPI [Worcester Polytechnic Institute] this year" to "This course was a waste of time and I learned [expletive deleted]." We therefore embarked on a study of student cognitive style distribution and its effect on course satisfaction and performance.

We found that in this particular course the cognitive style distribution was a moving target. Whereas in 1990 the *low differentiators*, who prefer well-defined tasks, predominated (40 percent problem solvers and 33 percent implementors), in 1991 and 1992 the number of *integrators*, who are most adaptable, increased at the expense of the *problem solvers*, who like well-defined tasks and open-ended solutions. In 1993, however, the *low remote associators*, who solve problems by persistence and logic rather than by intuitive leaps, were the predominant group. Thus, as we changed the course structure from year to year to accommodate the reactions of the previous year's class, we were playing to a new audience with different preferences. We believe that this cognitive style shift is somewhat unusual, because a similar study of a junior-level mechanical engineering course at WPI found that the cognitive style distribution matched that of mechanical engineering majors in general (Rogers, Barrett, and McNall, 1995). In the first-year biology course, the shifting distribution could be a result of the uncertainty of first-year students about their major, or a result of the volatility of public perception of the emerging field of biotechnology.

An examination of cognitive styles within groups in the general biology courses yielded the interesting result that cognitively homogeneous groups (containing one cognitive type) scored very high on group harmony but did not perform exceptionally well. Conversely, cognitively diverse groups were conflict-ridden, but as long as the conflict was not too extreme, they produced excellent work. We surmise that the same differences in perspective that cause diverse groups to argue are also responsible for excellent work when all points of view are considered in producing the final solution to the problem. Interestingly, however, group harmony seemed to be much more important than performance in determining a student's satisfaction with the course.

Armed with these data, we embarked on an experiment in restructuring (in terms of class organization) and partial destructuring (in terms of tasks) of the course. We destructured part of the curriculum, in a deliberate and ordered way, by starting with structured tasks and moving toward relatively unstructured ones. We deliberately formed cognitively diverse groups, and supplied them with Peer Learning Assistants (PLAs) to defuse group conflict. For one class period each week, students met privately in their groups with their PLA. In the scheduled in-class meeting, the agenda consisted of either deciding how to tackle the newly assigned project or editing the required first draft of the project nearing completion. Each PLA was responsible for up to three groups, having at least one formal meeting per week with each group in the conference section. At their discretion and that of their groups, PLAs often met with their groups outside of class, and were on call for after-hours assistance. The PLAs' job description clearly stated that they were not to function as group leaders, nor as peer tutors. Their job was to facilitate group process and group dynamics: to orient and assist the students in tackling complex, relatively ill-defined, open-ended tasks; to identify problems in group dynamics early, before they became nasty; and to help students resolve problems through open communication. Results of the PLA experiment have been positive: group harmony is as good in cognitively diverse groups with PLAs as it was in cognitively homogeneous groups without PLAs; satisfaction has improved; and performance is considerably better. At last it seems that we have identified the elements of structure necessary to create a successful course.

Simultaneously with these structural evolutions the number of faculty available to teach the course declined from two to one, and the student enrollment climbed from 35 in 1989 to 145 in 1995. Faculty productivity became a major problem with the cooperative learning format, because the out-of-class projects assigned required extensive faculty input working one-on-one with student groups, mainly to solve dynamics problems. The use of PLAs has enabled the continuation of active learning in a format that is very close to the original. Furthermore, the presence of a PLA seems to help students feel connected and cared about even in a large class. The PLA system improves group performance both by enabling and enforcing a draft–revise–final version system of preparing group reports, and by helping students to appreciate and use the diverse cognitive gifts of their peers. Written reports from PLAs indicate that they also find facilitating the cooperative learning activities personally beneficial. Among many positive outcomes, PLAs report learning how to help others, how to approach problems and think about alternative solutions, and how to better manage time. In addition, PLAs report improvement in their own academic performance (Groccia and Miller, 1996).

Issues and Questions: What Might Go Wrong

Criticisms of active learning often revolve around issues of structure, or more accurately, poor structure or lack of structure. As part of an overall institutional assessment program, Truman State University (formerly Northeast Missouri State University) interviewed students regarding their perceptions of the benefits and disadvantages of active learning ("Interview Project Report," 1994).

While students had positive things to say about active learning, most statements about its disadvantages related to issues of structure. Lack of adequate structure, focus, directions, or time; unequal participation; perception of active learning as busy work; lack of incentive to participate; unfair grading/evaluation techniques; and difficulty in completing group work out of class were listed as problems limiting the effectiveness of active learning.

The dynamic of interpersonal relationships in cooperative learning groups represents a potential source of conflict, even in carefully structured groups (Miller, Trimbur, and Wilkes, 1994; Hackman and Morris, 1975). Successful completion and quality of group tasks are heavily dependent upon a harmonious working relationship among group members. Students may not have much experience working in groups and can have inaccurate expectations of the roles and responsibilities of group members. Lack of individual responsibility on the part of group members is another potential source of difficulty. Even when the instructor takes appropriate courses of action to encourage individual accountability, conflict can arise when students have different levels of motivation and interest in task completion. Mechanisms for dealing with group conflicts should be shared with students at the outset of the course. Otherwise, highly motivated students will compensate for less-motivated group members by doing more than their share of work, and will rightfully resent having to do so to protect their grade. We do not recommend reconstituting groups, both because it disrupts other groups and because it is an option that is not usually available in the working world. A group can sometimes be effectively split into subgroups. An alternative is to establish a formal process modeled on a personnel action, through which an uncommitted group member may be "fired" from a group. Such a process can include written warnings, written documentation of problems and attempted solutions, and a review and approval by the professor. Using this method, the teacher must have a plan for options available to the fired student for completing the work of the course.

Conclusions and Remaining Questions

The degree of structure is a core issue to consider when attempting to create successful active learning approaches. Manipulation of the structure of course requirements, learning activities, tasks, and evaluation procedures greatly impacts student satisfaction and performance. The effect of structure, however, is influenced and mediated by many factors. Cognitive style is one of many manifestations of student diversity that contribute to different individual and group experiences in any active learning situation.

Structuring learning environments based on student characteristics raises important ethical and philosophical questions. The most basic question is, Should student characteristics be matched to teaching/learning activities "with malice aforethought," or should groups be formed and learning tasks designed blindly, without such considerations? Is "sorting by chance" a more democratic and equitable way to structure learning opportunities than using a variable such as cognitive style (which can be considered, to some degree, theoretical and experimental)?

By singling out one student characteristic, are others ignored that may be equally or more important? Perhaps the variable used to structure learning activities is not the one that is most directly related to student learning. The choice of characteristic may favor certain students, or groups of students, in terms of the quality of their learning and resulting evaluation and grade outcomes. Is it feasible to take into account all student characteristics that influence learning when designing a course?

Manipulating learning situations also raises philosophical and ethical issues. One such question emerges when deciding whether to form groups in a way that ensures that group members get along (by homogeneous cognitive style), or in a way that optimizes performance (cognitively mixed). Matching task type to cognitive style seems to increase student comfort and satisfaction but might not provide the challenge and cognitive disequilibrium that enhances learning. Should a faculty member (especially a nontenured one) risk student wrath, and possibly low student evaluations, by heterogeneously grouping them according to characteristics that may increase conflict and interpersonal tension yet result in higher quality performance? Conversely, is it ethically or legally defensible to deliberately create groups in which satisfaction is expected to be high but less learning may take place?

These questions highlight the difficulty of creating the perfect course (Miller, Wilkes, and Cheetham, 1993). Tailoring course structure to accommodate the strengths of one type of student may do so at the expense of another, or at the risk of decreasing satisfaction, group harmony, or performance. Manipulation of course structure to improve learning is not an easy task. Mixing the nature of learning tasks and instructional approaches within a course, and of subtasks within tasks, may be a solution to the challenges presented by student diversity. In any case, faculty must be cognizant of the impact of structure on successful course development. At the same time, identification and awareness of student characteristics that may influence the effectiveness of these efforts should also be taken into account. The interplay and symbiosis of these issues should be thoughtfully considered when attempting to structure an active learning class.

References

Blizek, W. L., Jackson, K., and LaVoie, J. C. "Short Course vs. Conventional Structures for Teaching Philosophy." *The Journal of Experimental Education,* 1974, 43 (1), 25–33.

Bloom, B. S. (ed.). *Taxonomy of Educational Objectives: The Classification of Educational Goals.* New York: Longman, 1956.

Bonwell, C. C., and Eison, J. A. *Active Learning: Creating Excitement in the Classroom.* ASHE-ERIC Higher Education Report No. 1. Washington, D. C.: George Washington University, School of Education and Human Development, 1991.

Booth-Butterfield, M. "Stifle or Stimulate? The Effects of Communication Task Structure on Apprehensive and Non-Apprehensive Students." *Communication Education,* 1986, 35, 337–348.

Claxton, C. S., and Murrill, P. H. *Learning Styles: Implications for Improving Educational Practices.* ASHE-ERIC Higher Education Report no. 4. College Station, TX: Association for the Study of Higher Education, 1987.

Cronbach, L. J. "The Two Disciplines of Scientific Psychology." *American Psychologist,* 1957, *12,* 671–684.

Cronbach, L. J., and Snow, R. E. *Aptitudes and Instructional Methods.* New York: Irvington, 1977.

Daly, J., and Buss, A. "The Transitory Causes of Audience Anxiety." In J. Daly and J. McCroskey (eds.), *Avoiding Communication: Communication Apprehension, Reticence, and Shyness.* Thousand Oaks, Calif.: Sage, 1984.

Domino, G. "Interactive Effects of Achievement Orientation and Teaching Style on Academic Achievement." *Journal of Educational Psychology,* 1971, *62,* 427–431.

Felder, R. M. "We Never Said It Would be Easy." *Chemical Engineering Education,* Winter 1995, pp. 32–33.

Glaser, R. "Ten Untenable Assumptions of College Instruction." *Educational Researcher,* 1968, *49,* 154–159.

Gordon, G., and Morse, E. "Creative Potential and Organizational Structure." *Journal of Academic Management,* 1969, *11* (3), 37–49.

Groccia, J. E., and Miller, J. E. "Collegiality in the Classroom: The Use of Peer Learning Assistants in Cooperative Learning in Introductory Biology." *Innovation in Higher Education,* 1996, *21* (2).

Gronlund, N. E., and Linn, R. L. *Measurement and Evaluation in Teaching.* Old Tappan, N.J.: Macmillan, 1990.

Hackman, J. R., and Morris, C. G. "Group Process and Group Performance Effectiveness: A Review and Proposed Integration." In L. Berkowitz (ed.), *Advances in Experimental Social Psychology.* Orlando, Fla.: Academic Press, 1975.

"Interview Project Report." Report of the University Assessment Committee, Northeast Missouri State University, Kirksville, February 1994.

Mednick, S. "The Associative Basis of the Creative Process." In S. Mednick and M. Mednick (eds.), *Research in Personality.* Austin, Tex.: Holt, Rinehart and Winston, 1963.

Miller, J. E., and Cheetham, R. D. "Teaching Freshmen to Think: Active Learning in Introductory Biology." *Bioscience,* 1990, *40,* 388–391.

Miller, J. E., Trimbur, J., and Wilkes, J. M. "Group Dynamics: Understanding Group Success and Failure in Collaborative Learning." In K. Bosworth and S. J. Hamilton (eds.), *Collaborative Learning: Underlying Processes and Effective Techniques.* New Directions for Teaching and Learning, no. 59. San Francisco: Jossey-Bass, 1994.

Miller, J. E., Wilkes, J., and Cheetham, R. D. "Tradeoffs in Student Satisfaction: Is the "Perfect" Course an Illusion?" *Journal on Excellence in College Teaching,* 1993, *4,* 27–47.

Perry, W. G., Jr. *Forms of Intellectual and Ethical Development in the College Years: A Scheme.* Austin, Tex.: Holt, Rinehart and Winston, 1970.

Pilkonis, P. "The Behavioral Consequences of Shyness." *Journal of Personality,* 1977, *45,* 596–611.

Rogers, J. J., Barrett, S., and McNall, M. "Learning Styles at WPI." Unpublished Interactive Qualifying Project, Worcester Polytechnic Institute, 1995.

Shaw, R. A. "The Performance of Students with a Range of Preferences for Structure in Three Non-Traditional College Programs." Unpublished master's thesis, University of Chicago, 1975.

Smith, D.E.P., Wood, R. L., Downer, J. W., and Raygor, A. L. "Reading Improvements as a Function of Student Personality and Teaching Method." *Journal of Educational Psychology,* 1956, *47,* 47–59.

The American Heritage Dictionary, Second College Edition. Boston: Houghton Mifflin, 1985.

JUDITH E. MILLER is associate professor of biology and biotechnology at Worcester Polytechnic Institute in Worcester, Massachusetts.

JAMES E. GROCCIA is the director of the Program for Excellence in Teaching and adjunct associate professor of psychology at the University of Missouri-Columbia.

JOHN M. WILKES is associate professor of sociology at Worcester Polytechnic Institute.

The traditional lecture can be enhanced by including active learning designed to further course goals of learning knowledge, developing skills, or fostering attitudes.

Enhancing the Lecture: Revitalizing a Traditional Format

Charles C. Bonwell

During the past twenty years a number of educational authorities and blue ribbon commissions have called for introducing active learning into our classrooms. The resulting changes have been particularly evident in the health professions, which found that traditional lectures emphasizing the memorization of information ill-prepared students for clinical settings, in which they were asked to demonstrate sophisticated communication and problem-solving skills. To meet this need, the American Association of Colleges of Pharmacy, for instance, challenged its member institutions to develop an outcomes-based curriculum utilizing active learning that would provide students with the skills necessary to practice pharmacy effectively in the twenty-first century. In response, the faculty at the Saint Louis College of Pharmacy, among others, has begun to significantly change its educational objectives and teaching strategies in the classroom in order to explicitly teach towards outcomes and then assess the effectiveness of that effort ("Background Paper II," 1993). These changes, and others like them, have created a tension in higher education.

For example, a recent discussion on the Internet erupted into a heated debate as usually sedate college professors vehemently attacked or vigorously defended the traditional lecture. Unfortunately, the protagonists relied more on singular personal experience to defend their stances than on knowledge of the pertinent, available research. Such emotional arguments, while not uncommon, serve little purpose other than generating ill-will based on a false dichotomy. Lectures, whether good or bad, depend on situational context, instructor skill, and course objectives.

More-dispassionate observers of the educational process would argue that to increase their effectiveness it is important to understand both the advantages *and* the limitations of the lecture. Cashin (1985, pp. 2–3) states that lectures have the following strengths:

1. Effective lecturers can communicate the intrinsic interest of a subject through their enthusiasm.
2. Lectures can present material not otherwise available to students.
3. Lectures can be specially organized to meet the needs of particular audiences.
4. Lectures can present large amounts of information.
5. Lectures can be presented to large audiences.
6. Lecturers can model how professionals work through disciplinary questions or problems.
7. Lectures allow the instructor maximum control of the learning experience.
8. Lectures present little risk for students.
9. Lectures appeal to those who learn by listening.

Cashin (pp. 3–4) goes on to point out the disadvantages of traditional lectures (fifty or seventy-five minutes of teacher talk):

1. Lectures fail to provide instructors with feedback about the extent of student learning. (Thinking in terms of how much the student is learning as opposed to how much material has been presented is a fundamental and necessary shift in perspective.)
2. In lectures students are often passive because there is no mechanism to ensure that they are intellectually engaged with the material.
3. Students' attention wanes quickly after fifteen to twenty-five minutes.
4. Information tends to be forgotten quickly when students are passive.
5. Lectures presume that all students learn at the same pace and are at the same level of understanding.
6. Lectures are not suited for teaching higher orders of thinking such as application, analysis, synthesis, or evaluation; for teaching motor skills; or for influencing attitudes or values.
7. Lectures are not well suited for teaching complex, abstract material.
8. Lectures require effective speakers.
9. Lectures emphasize learning by listening, which is a disadvantage for students who have other learning styles.

An understanding of these strengths and limitations provides insight into how we might improve our teaching.

For instance, systematically incorporating brief active learning strategies into lectures minimizes many of the weaknesses of the lecture approach. Discussion questions; short, in-class writing assignments; and formative (ungraded) quizzes quickly provide feedback about student comprehension of the material being presented. Moreover, these activities keep students from becoming passive, and if interspersed at appropriate times, keep student attention focused. Research also suggests that active learning techniques are more effective for teaching higher-order thinking skills and are useful when trying to change student attitudes or to motivate students (McKeachie, Pintrich, Yi-Guang, and Smith, 1986). Finally, the use of differing active learning techniques reaches a broad range of student learning styles. The use of these activities, then, can significantly enhance our lectures.

For purposes of discussion, an *enhanced lecture* is defined as a series of short, mini-lectures punctuated by specific active learning events designed to meet class objectives. Using this model, the enhanced lecture could fall anywhere on the active learning continuum, depending on the complexity and frequency of the strategies used. A simple enhanced lecture could involve two to three pauses during the lecture to allow students to compare notes or ask questions. Those instructors who are familiar and comfortable with more complex strategies might choose to incorporate into the class period lengthy group activities focused on skill development, punctuated with brief mini-lectures that summarize a previous activity or create a transition for the next activity. Again, the extent to which these active learning strategies are incorporated into the lecture depends on the course objectives and the instructor's teaching style. As in many situations, more is not necessarily better.

The enhanced lecture will have a beneficial impact upon students. A number of research studies have shown that active learning is preferable to traditional lecture if the instructor's goal is to develop higher-order thinking or change student attitudes (Bonwell and Eison, 1991). The power of interaction in a classroom is nicely illustrated by the following story. A physics professor, a traditional lecturer, at Truman State University (formerly Northeast Missouri State University) had serious doubts about the efficacy of active learning and believed that he could challenge its proponents' claims through a rigorous, quantitative study. Accordingly, in his introductory physics course he taught two sections, to provide both an experimental and control group. In the control group, the professor lectured for several minutes, then asked students to work individually on problem worksheets for twenty minutes. The final portion of the class involved the professor solving the problems in front of the classroom, encouraging students to contribute their answers where appropriate. Conversely, in the experimental class, after a brief lecture to introduce concepts, the students worked in small groups on the problem worksheets for twenty minutes while the instructor moved between groups answering questions that arose. For the next five to ten minutes, student groups shared their answers with the class. Finally, if there was still confusion about the problems, the instructor would provide his solution. All other parameters of the class were the same (homework, quizzes, exams, and labs).

At the end of the course, the instructor analyzed pretest and posttest scores, student performance on a standardized physics examination, and results of an attitudinal survey given at the beginning, middle, and end of the semester. He concluded that there was no statistical difference in the performance of the two groups with regard to their understanding of Newtonian mechanics. He did find, however, a significant difference (both statistically and educationally) in how the students reacted to the course. The motivation level of the control group remained the same throughout the semester while the motivation level of the experimental group rose approximately 50 percent during the course of the semester. These students "showed a great deal of enthusiasm" in the course and reported "having fun" (Samiullah, in press). Because student performance stayed the same, the change in student attitude persuaded the instructor to act on the evidence of his own experiment. He has changed his teaching style in the introductory course to include active learning (Samiullah, in press).

Planning and Structuring the Enhanced Lecture

Before examining active learning strategies that are appropriate for the enhanced lecture, at least three assumptions must be articulated: (1) we have done the preliminary groundwork for assessing the course as to the appropriate levels of knowledge, skills, and attitudes that we wish our students to demonstrate (see Chapter One); (2) we are knowledgeable and skillful lecturers who understand the various forms that a lecture can take to promote effective communication; and (3) our mini-lectures will never be more than fifteen to twenty minutes long. (This assumption is based on research that suggests that students cannot effectively assimilate material beyond that time frame.) Given these assumptions, the following questions are appropriate:

How does this activity meet my course objectives? In order to select specific active learning techniques that further our course objectives, let's focus on the three questions raised in Chapter One: (1) What do I want my students to know? (2) What do I want my students to do? and (3) What do I want my students to feel? Used in conjunction with Bloom's taxonomy of educational objectives (Bloom, 1956) or with an understanding of the macro and micro skills inherent in our disciplinary processes, these three questions provide a useful blueprint for developing specific active learning activities in class.

What do I want my students to know? Bloom's first two levels of thinking—knowledge and comprehension—are the principle focus of many professors in the classroom. Within this model, *knowledge* means the information (facts, rules, or principles) that students must recall in order to practice higher-order thinking skills. By asking students the familiar questions *who, what, when, where,* and *how,* we can quickly ascertain whether or not they have learned the information as we intended. Perhaps more important, we want to know whether students truly understand, or comprehend, the material being presented. Can they organize and select facts and ideas presented in a meaningful way? Can they describe the concept in their own words? This assessment is particularly important with novice students, who often can regurgitate facts and figures or who have memorized formulas without really understanding their meaning. (If you have not had this experience, ask a beginning student what the words *democracy* or *velocity* mean.) One of the central roles that active learning can play in the enhanced lecture, therefore, is to provide a mechanism to see how students understand the lecture. Specific activities that might be included in the lecture are the pause procedure, short writes, Think-Pair-Share, formative quizzes, lecture summaries and Classroom Assessment Techniques.

The Pause Procedure. Two factors underlie the pause procedure's effectiveness. First, stopping the lecture every thirteen to eighteen minutes allows the students to do something else, thus dealing with the physiological and psychological responses that keep them from listening effectively for longer periods of time. Presumably, short breaks allow people to return to peak listening efficiency. Second, having students compare notes makes good sense. Two people working together are likely to take better notes than one person working alone, and experience indeed supports this assumption. Students inevitably discover that they learn something from someone else's notes. To break the predictability of the pause procedure, it is advisable to mix this technique with others, such as short writes, opportunities for questions, and so forth.

Short Writes. Punctuating a lecture with short writing assignments is a powerful way to assess the degree to which students understand presented material. For instance, the "one-minute paper," advocated by Angelo and Cross (1993), can be as simple as asking, "What was the most important thing you learned during this class?" or "What questions remained unanswered?" Within the framework of an enhanced lecture we could present three questions or instructions at evenly spaced intervals, such as the following: "What was the main idea presented in this portion of the lecture?" "What are some of the major concepts associated with today's topic?" and "Describe the concept of _____ in your own words." The resulting short writes could be submitted to the instructor or they could form the basis for class discussions. (On a practical note, one-minute papers usually take three to five minutes to implement.)

Think-Pair-Share. Think-Pair-Share is a widely used technique that serves many purposes. In its simplest form, two students discuss together for two to three minutes what would be an appropriate answer to a question that has been asked. They then share their results in a large class discussion. If time permits, it is more effective to have students write down their individual answers to the question prior to talking in pairs. Writing forces each student to attempt an initial response to the question, which they can then clarify and expand as they collaborate. Writing then talking about their answers can take five to ten minutes depending on the question's complexity. An extension of this format is to have two pairs join each other and compare answers.

Think-Pair-Share is particularly effective because it can work in classes of any size to get students involved. It is also an effective way to deal with a student's reluctance to answer questions from the instructor, particularly at the beginning of the semester, before rapport and trust have been established. Students are much more willing to share joint answers than to be held individually accountable for their responses. This is particularly true in large classes where many students are intimidated, fearing to "look stupid" in front of their peers.

Formative Quizzes. Formative—that is, ungraded—quizzes are used to easily and efficiently determine how students comprehend material. Using the same types of questions that would normally be used on major examinations, the instructor places questions on the board or an overhead projector, giving students an appropriate time to respond. (Complex essays could be broken into component parts.) If the question entails multiple choice, students can raise their hands in agreement as each prompt is featured. With this approach, instructors quickly determine how most students understand what has been presented. Misunderstood material warrants a clarifying discussion. In addition to determining comprehension, formative quizzes educate students about the kinds of questions they will be expected to answer on the major exams. This preview can lessen student anxiety by making the instructor's expectations clear. Conversely, it can show students problem areas that warrant further study.

Lecture Summaries. Students can better synthesize course material if they are provided with specific opportunities to summarize lectures during class. As previously suggested, this opportunity for synthesis can be done informally by short writes or by having small groups of students share notes. A more formal approach is the guided lecture (Kelly and Holmes, 1979), which consists of the following steps: After presenting the objectives of the lecture, the instructor asks students to put their pencils down and listen carefully to a lecture that is approximately one-half of the class period. The students' goal is to determine the major concepts presented and to remember as much supporting data as possible. For five minutes at the end of the lecture students are asked to write down all of the presentation they can recall. Working in small groups, students then construct a complete set of lecture notes, using the instructor as a resource when necessary. Kelly and Holmes are convinced that the approach improves students' listening skills and creates a set of notes superior to those taken by most individuals.

Classroom Assessment Techniques. Three classroom assessment techniques outlined by Angelo and Cross (1993, pp. 126–147) can assess students' recall of information presented in the classroom. Focused listing, which could be used at any time during the course of a lecture, is designed to see whether students recall the most important points associated with a particular topic (for example, create a list of the advantages of both the North and the South going into the Civil War). A second approach provides students with an empty or partially filled outline of the lecture and asks them to fill in the blanks in a limited amount of time. A third technique consists of a two-dimensional table with rows and columns that are used to organize information and illustrate relationships (for example, list one major political, economic, and social consequence of World War II for each of the countries shown in Exhibit 3.1).

These techniques can be individual or group assignments depending on the instructor's goals and preferences.

What do I want students to do (skills)? Traditionally, in the classroom faculty have placed most of their emphasis on recounting disciplinary content. Skill development has been relegated to laboratory or homework assignments. Experience tells us, however, that students often need explicit coaching in the

Exhibit 3.1. Consequences of World War II

	Political	Economic	Social
Great Britain			
Russia			
Germany			
Japan			

classroom before they can effectively develop those skills outside the class-room. (As an example, can you think back to a class when as a student you were certain you could do the math or science problem illustrated, until you went home and actually tried to do it—and found you didn't have a clue? Most of us can.) *Explicitly* is the key word here. Although many of us believe that students learn specific skills as we model them in front of a classroom, most students cannot learn the skill unless they actually go through the process.

Using Bloom's Taxonomy to Develop Activities at an Appropriate Level

When I ask faculty to list those skills that they are teaching in the classroom, "thinking" tops the list. When I push the issue further and ask what strategies they use to teach thinking in the classroom, there is less agreement. Traditionally, we have relied on problem sets or written assignments outside the classroom; inside the classroom we often focus on clarifying the lecture material. Although most of us want to help our students enhance their ability to think, we are uncertain how to approach this task explicitly. Specific active learning techniques structured around questions using Bloom's taxonomy (Bloom, 1956) is one way to meet this challenge.

One of the keys to constructing exercises designed to promote thinking is to ensure that the questions asked are at an appropriate level. As shown in Exhibit 3.2, the Maryland State Department of Education (McTighe, 1985) developed an extremely useful guide to help instructors frame questions that can be used to generate discussions or as prompts for active learning exercises.

Bloom's original work is another rich source for examples of questions at varying levels that cut across disciplines.

Many general activities that are suitable for an enhanced lecture in any discipline—such as individual short writes, small or large group activities, jour-nals, formative quizzes, and so on—could be organized around the questions presented in Exhibit 3.2. More-specific activities are found in Angelo and Cross (1993), which classifies all of its Classroom Assessment Techniques according to Bloom's taxonomy. For instance, the Pro and Con Grid (p. 168), which lists advantages and disadvantages of any concept, helps students develop analytical and evaluative skills. The Defining Features Matrix (p. 164), which asks students to compare and contrast features of related items or concepts, is a structured analytical activity applicable in any discipline. All of these approaches can help students explicitly to enhance their thinking.

What disciplinary skills do I want them to know? Another way to approach the development of skills in a classroom is while planning the course to ask the question, What skills from my discipline do I want students in this course to acquire? A global response to this question might be, "I want my students to understand the scientific method [or issue analysis or decision making, and so on]." This response leads, however, to even more difficult questions: What are the component parts of this skill and how do I teach them explicitly? What skills are appropriate for this class, given the level of the course? Recognizing that the development of a skill is a repetitive process, we must ask, How many times and in what different contexts must students have the opportunity to practice this skill? How will I assess whether or not students have acquired the skill at an acceptable level of proficiency? In the limited time available in any given class period, what content am I willing to give up to develop this skill? These questions, at the heart of ability-based education, usually overwhelm newcomers to the concept of explicitly teaching skills. Many instructors simply do not know where to begin.

The answer to this dilemma is to start small, working with a few carefully structured exercises that illustrate a skill that you consider crucial for students who are studying your discipline to possess. For instance, as a historian I decided that issue analysis was central to my discipline. I wanted my students to read an article or historical passage and be able to answer the following basic questions:

What is the issue in this piece?
What is the author's conclusion with regard to the issue?
What are the main arguments provided by the author?
What evidence is presented? Is the evidence credible?
Are there ambiguous statements in the text?
Do you agree with the author's conclusion? Why or why not?

It should be pointed out that I had never been taught this concept or process explicitly when I was a student at any level. (For an extended discussion of issue analysis, see Browne and Keeley, 1994.)

My first attempt at introducing these skills was a disaster. In an introductory class for first-year students, after lecturing briefly over some now-forgotten concept, I told the students we were going to answer some questions about the associated reading that had been assigned the previous class period. I then

Exhibit 3.2. Guide for Framing Questions

Knowledge: Identification and recall of information

Who, what, when, where, how _____ ?

Describe _____ .

Comprehension: Organization and selection of facts and ideas

Retell _____ in your own words.

Application: Use of facts, rules, and principles

How is _____ an example of _____ ?

How is _____ related to _____ ?

Why is _____ significant?

Analysis: Separation of a whole into component parts

What are the parts or features of _____ ?

Classify _____ according to _____ .

Outline/diagram _____ .

How does _____ compare/contrast with _____ ?

What evidence can you list for _____ ?

Synthesis: Combination of ideas to form a new whole

What would you predict/infer from _____ ?

What ideas can you add to _____ ?

How would you create/design a new _____ ?

What might happen if you combined _____ ?

What solutions would you suggest for _____ ?

Evaluation: Development of opinions, judgments, or decisions

Do you agree with/that _____ ?

What do you think about _____ ?

What is the most important _____ ?

Place the following in priority order: _____ .

How would you decide about _____ ?

What criteria would you use to assess _____ ?

Source: Adapted from McTighe, 1985.

gave the students oral instructions about the eight questions I wanted them to answer, and asked them to work individually on the task for ten minutes. A large class discussion, I confidently declared, would follow.

Those experienced with active learning can only smile at the naivete of both my process and my expectations; no doubt they could predict the confusion and frustration that erupted in the classroom, forcing me to abandon the exercise. In the years since, I have learned to ponder the following questions before introducing any new strategy in class. These questions apply to the introduction of any skill, not just issue analysis.

Are my expectations realistic with regard to class level? In this instance, I overwhelmed students with analytical tasks that were beyond their experience, and for some, beyond their cognitive abilities. After working on this skill at least once a week, however, by the end of the semester most students could confidently identify the issue, the author's conclusion, and most of the major arguments being presented. Some could consistently provide a more sophisticated and complete analysis involving evidence, ambiguity, and so on.

How can I ensure that students are prepared for the exercise/discussion? Ensuring student preparedness is a concern that faculty express again and again. The key is to create assignments that encourage student responsibility. These could include answering associated study questions, developing summaries, or solving problems that are turned in at the beginning of class. Although more draconian and time-consuming, announced quizzes lead to more careful preparation. (In my experience, pop quizzes rarely work because overly optimistic students readily assume that you will not give a quiz that day.) Finally, particularly if the material is complex, you could reproduce a key or representative section of the assignment on which to base student analysis and discussion.

How will I introduce the skill? Students must see how the skill should be performed. Usually this is a two-step process: first, the instructor models the skill so that students can see how an expert uses it; second, students attempt the skill in class, getting as much feedback as possible during their initial attempts. This method is strengthened if you can state criteria for what constitutes a good answer or if you are able to provide examples of other students (both good and bad, preferably from students not in the class).

How will I structure the exercise/problem? The issue analysis exercise described earlier was ineffectively structured. First, the instructions should have been written out and handed to students to facilitate understanding. Moreover, since it was the first time that students had encountered this skill, asking them to work in pairs would have been more productive than asking them to work individually. Together they would have generated better responses to the questions, and the resulting class discussion would have been more lively since they would have had collective responsibility for the answers given.

Are my expectations realistic with regard to time? As a rule of thumb, expect to use more time than you planned for the first run of an exercise: things won't go as expected, and you will have planned too much. In the issue analysis exercise, I presented students with far too many questions to respond to in the time allotted. Because it was the first time the class had been asked to engage in issue analysis, a more realistic expectation would have been to ask students to focus on one or two of the analytical questions (for instance, What is the issue and what is the author's conclusion?), perhaps spending three to five minutes writing an answer to the question, then turning to a partner for an additional five minutes to clarify their responses. Finally, the class as a whole, with the instructor facilitating the discussion, could have spent five to ten minutes on the topic. As the semester progressed, less time would be needed to review specific skills as students developed proficiency.

How will I assess that students have achieved proficiency in the skill? The key to assessing skills is to do it frequently (relying more on formative than on summative assessment), to provide criteria that are as complete as possible, and to have congruence between the skills you teach and the way you structure major tests. When instructors exhort students to "think" but issue multiple choice tests focused primarily on factual knowledge, students quickly perceive the disparity and spend their study time accordingly.

What do I want students to feel (attitudes)? Although faculty often do not consider student attitudes as central to planning their course, in most disciplines they are important. Many health professionals, for instance, perceive as crucial the ability to be empathetic towards clients. Their courses may place heavy emphasis on such techniques as role play, which is designed to foster greater understanding of cultural differences in their patients. Even if we do not see an immediate professional need, most of us would like students to appreciate our disciplines, to understand that they can be exciting, enjoyable, perhaps even fun. Too often in our drive to cover "the material," however, we forget to allow students opportunities to experience the joy of using our disciplinary techniques to gain an understanding of themselves and their environment. Two examples of instructors who address student attitudes will suffice. A cultural historian at a small liberal arts college integrates the lyrics of popular songs of a particular period with slides of events representative of the same period to evoke a visceral understanding of history. Similarly, a distinguished professor of chemistry at a major research institution enters the classroom wearing an outdated polyester coat. Casually he demonstrates the near indestructibility of the material (such as briskly rubbing the coat with a wire brush) while discussing the chemical composition of polymers. It is no accident that these two individuals have reputations at their institutions as outstanding teachers. Without sacrificing intellectual rigor, they work at making their subject matter come alive for students.

Creating the Enhanced Lecture

Before we can structure our enhanced lecture, we need to make a series of contextual and logistical decisions.

What are the physical limitations of the room? Fixed chairs or long rows of tables are just two of the many constraints that unknowing architects have placed on the use of active learning in many classrooms. The more that movement is restricted, the less ambitious can be our efforts. No matter what constraints exist, however, we can always use individual activities and work students in pairs.

How large is the class? Class size also determines what activities we can use in the classroom. In a large class not only do physical constraints hamper active learning, but the sheer numbers of students will limit our efforts as well. For instance, just getting students to break into appropriate groups can be daunting in a large class, although at least one professor overcame this problem by color-coding lecture hall seats. Also, we cannot hear from everyone even if we are working in groups; reports from representative groups can speed up the process. Finally, just the mechanics of handing out prompts for discussion (surveys, problems, and so on) or retrieving responses is a challenge in a large class. We must find ways to overcome these obstacles by using well-defined groups, streamlining reporting procedures, developing prompts on overheads, and so on.

How will my teaching style influence my choice of strategies? Each of us needs to reflect on those personal characteristics that affect our classroom teaching style so that we choose appropriate strategies. Some instructors, concerned about "losing control" of a discussion's direction or fearing that they cannot answer tangential questions, need structured, focused activities. Others, uncomfortable with the noise accompanying highly animated discussions, may need to rely on more-sedate activities such as formative quizzes or writing exercises. Still others find that the systematic planning that goes into a formal cooperative learning course does not fit their needs for flexibility and spontaneity. To be effective, therefore, we must select strategies congruent with who we are.

Where are we in the semester? (How familiar are my students with the material and the tactics?) Finally, we must consider the temporal issue of where in the semester we are. Early in the semester large group discussions are less effective than pairs because students hesitate to voice opinions in front of strangers. Similarly, if students are still learning basic concepts and associated vocabulary, they may resist engaging in a meaningful role play or analyzing a case study with any degree of sophistication. Our decisions on strategies, therefore, are always contextual.

For purposes of discussion, let's assume that we are teaching an introductory American history class to 150 first-year students. In the fifth week of the semester, our active learning based script for a presentation on the causes of the American revolution might be as follows (numbers represent allotted minutes):

[7] Formative quiz and discussion about key study terms to determine student understanding of the basic material [overhead transparency in large type].

[15] Mini-lecture on the political causes of the Revolution, with an emphasis on Locke's compact theory of government.

[10] Small-group discussion (two to three students each) analyzing the introduction to the Declaration of Independence, finding specific examples of the
compact theory [overhead transparency prompt].

[8] Large-group discussion for explication and clarification.

[7] Mini-lecture on the influence of the compact theory on contemporary
political thought.

[3] One-minute write: What questions do you still have about the compact
theory? Leave your responses in the box at the back of the room.

The most difficult part of implementing a new script is getting the timing right.
Experience dictates that one-minute writes take two to five minutes, Think-Pair-
Share needs ten minutes or more for complex tasks, and large group discussions
provide the greatest time flexibility because instructors control the interaction.
In addition, most of us plan too much in any given time frame. So, if the timing
is thrown off because students do not understand a concept or because a topic
generates significant discussion that you want to continue, substitute a less complex strategy somewhere further along. For instance, in the active learning based
script presented earlier, if the initial discussion went longer than intended (fifteen rather than seven minutes), the analysis of the Declaration of Independence
could become totally a large-group discussion shorter in length. Finally, if the
events planned do not create the experience envisioned, an instructor can always
fall back on Plan B, which for most of us is to lecture. With practice, the ability
to modify activities as the class progresses simply becomes routine.

For those who are starting to use active learning in their classrooms, the
enhanced lecture provides maximum flexibility. It can be fashioned to meet a
wide variety of course objectives in any discipline, even under the most trying
of circumstances. Moreover, given the number of options available to us, the
enhanced lecture can also meet the personal needs of most instructors, regardless of their teaching style. The key to its success is to think carefully about
what you want to accomplish, to reflect on the context of your classroom, and
then to plan structured activities that meet your goals.

For More Information

For a summary of the research on active learning, see Bonwell and Eison (1991,
pp. 8–10). If you would like to review other research pertaining to lectures, consider the following: although published more than twenty years ago, perhaps the
most complete work is Bligh (1974), which details research on the acquisition
of information and the effectiveness of specific lecture techniques. A more recent
work by Penner (1984) has an extensive section on classroom presentation. In
an excellent article that demonstrates the scholarship of teaching at its best,
Chilcoat (1989) offers specific recommendations to improve clarity based on the
findings of 104 studies. There are also a number of articles or chapters in jour-
nals and books devoted to teaching. For example, see periodic articles in *College
Teaching* or books by Brookfield (1995), Davis (1993), and others.

References

Angelo, T. A., and Cross, K. P. *Classroom Assessment Techniques: A Handbook for College Teachers* (2nd ed.). San Francisco: Jossey-Bass, 1993.

"Background Paper II: Entry-Level, Curricular Outcomes, Curricular Content and Educational Process." *American Journal of Pharmaceutical Education,* 1993, *57,* 85–96.

Bligh, D. A. *What's the Use of Lectures?* New York: Penguin Books, 1974.

Bloom, B. S. (ed.). *Taxonomy of Educational Objectives: The Classification of Educational Goals.* New York: Longman, 1956.

Bonwell, C. C., and Eison, J. A. *Active Learning: Creating Excitement in the Classroom.* ASHE-ERIC Higher Education Report No. 1. Washington, D. C.: George Washington University, School of Education and Human Development, 1991.

Brookfield, S. D. *Becoming a Critically Reflective Teacher.* San Francisco: Jossey-Bass, 1995.

Browne, N. M., and Keeley, S. M. *Asking the Right Questions: A Guide to Critical Thinking.* Englewood Cliffs, N.J.: Prentice Hall, 1994.

Cashin, W. E. *Improving Lectures.* Idea Paper No. 14. Manhattan: Kansas State University, Center for Faculty Evaluation and Development, 1985.

Chilcoat, C. W. "Instructional Behaviors for Clearer Presentations in the Classroom." *Instructional Science,* 1989, *18* (4), 289–314.

Davis, J. R. *Better Teaching, More Learning: Strategies for Success in Postsecondary Settings.* Phoenix, Ariz.: Oryx Press, 1993.

Kelly, B. W., and Holmes, J. "The Guided Lecture Procedure." *Journal of Reading,* 1979, *22,* 602–604.

McKeachie, W. J., Pintrich, P. R., Yi-Guang, L., and Smith, D.A.F. *Teaching and Learning in the College Classroom: A Review of the Research Literature.* Ann Arbor: Regents of the University of Michigan, 1986.

McTighe, J. "Questioning for Quality Thinking." Mimeographed. Baltimore: Maryland State Department of Education, Division of Instruction, 1985.

Penner, J. G. *Why Many College Teachers Cannot Lecture.* Springfield, Ill.: Thomas, 1984.

Samiullah, M. "Effect of In-Class Student-Student Interaction on the Learning of Physics in a College Physics Course." *American Journal of Physics,* in press.

CHARLES C. BONWELL, *coauthor of* Active Learning: Creating Excitement in the Classroom, *has conducted active learning workshops on more than fifty college and university campuses.*

Writing is a useful tool for helping students achieve the distance they need to begin to critically evaluate their own work.

Encouraging Self-Assessment: Writing as Active Learning

Eric H. Hobson

Bonwell and Eison (1991, p. 2) define active learning as anything that "involves students in doing things and thinking about the things they are doing." This definition is particularly useful because it focuses on the metacognitive aspects of learning. Thinking about our actions allows us to reflect on them and to postulate alternatives which in turn allow us opportunities to improve our future performance. Metacognition—thinking about our thoughts and actions—is the essence of active and independent learning. If this definition of active learning holds as well as I believe it does, then writing is about as holistic an active-learning endeavor as one can experience.

As a result of the active learning and the writing-across-the-curriculum movements, writing-to-learn activities (in and out of the classroom), as well as more traditional writing assignments, are among strategies often discussed for encouraging and facilitating active learning in the classroom (Young and Fulwiler, 1986). For the most part, however, these activities involve students at the front end of their learning processes, when they are busy discovering and exploring ideas. Activities such as short writing assignments, brainstorming activities, keeping a journal, and summarizing lectures are for the most part invention activities; they lead to early stages of text production. These activities provide students with algorithms they can use, for instance, to create associations between a course's primary concepts, which are often abstract, and the

The author wishes to thank Chuck Bonwell and Kenneth Schafermeyer, St. Louis College of Pharmacy, for the insights, collegiality, support, and materials that provided much of the basis for this chapter; and Carla McDonough, Eastern Illinois University, for her probing reading of and commentary on many drafts of the manuscript.

concrete facts that support or illustrate the concepts. Activities that use writing encourage students to engage in analytical and synthetic activity, both of which are higher-order thought processes (Bloom, 1956; Camposella, 1993). These benefits are important because they help students begin to assimilate new ideas into their existing frames of reference in ways that allow them to usefully integrate the resulting knowledge.

Whereas the literature on writing within the active learning classroom most often focuses on initial stages in the learning process (Bonwell and Eison, 1991, pp. 35–37), this chapter explores writing's usefulness as an active learning tool at the later stages of the learning process. Particularly, this chapter looks at how writing helps students develop the difficult but necessary skill of achieving the critical distance they need to make accurate evaluations—the ability to step away from and subsequently assess their action. Most of this discussion centers specifically around the demanding task of critically evaluating one's own writing in order to begin re(en)visioning it in more effective forms.

The Power of Why

As all parents know, children's desires to know why things happen the way they do and why things work are insatiable. They want explanations that help them make sense of their experiences—they want to learn (Vygotsky, 1962). Although the incessant why can be annoying, parents are usually tolerant because they can witness the value of these questions that reflect, for instance, developing analytic and synthetic thought processes. In the process of asking why the child gains a more mature knowledge base. At the same time, parents gain insight into how the child makes sense of reality, an insight that offers parents opportunities to provide helpful feedback. What results is a true win-win situation.

The power of why as an essential element in the learning process is not lost on adults. In formal education settings, however, these important questions often are shunted aside, moved to the periphery, suggesting in the process that why questions—questions that require explanation and explication—are ancillary, not central to learning. Often teachers are so thoroughly immersed in the workings of their discipline that the answers to students' why questions seem blatantly obvious, so transparent as to be hardly worth acknowledging—especially when teachers feel pressured to mention other information not yet presented. Likewise, in the apparent rush to receive discrete "facts," students fall into a trap of thinking that what is important is that they can recall information, not that they really understand its workings. In this scenario, everyone loses.

Creating a classroom environment that encourages students to actively develop their abilities to meaningfully self-assess their actions requires teachers to foreground the importance of asking others and oneself why and of answering those questions objectively (Dewey, 1963). Because this metacognitive process requires students to slow down their usual rapid-fire stream of thoughts and opinions in order to allow them the time and intellectual space required to analyze, synthesize, and evaluate their efforts, self-assessment is not a process that students master easily. Writing is highly effective in teaching this kind of reflection because, by its very physicalness, it is a process much slower than thinking (Matsuhashi, 1981). Writing also provides a permanent record that one may return to repeatedly, which makes it easier to analyze and evaluate than is possible using the fleeting and intangible medium of thought. Repeated opportunities to engage in written self-assessment offer students the use of a powerful set of tools by which to make sense of their experiences.

Why Self-Evaluation Skills are Critical

When it comes to learning to express one's thoughts in writing, few students get the opportunity to develop a metacognitive approach that enables them to reread their performances, analyze them, synthesize possible options, and evaluate their relative merits in order to plan an appropriate response. As such, we should not be surprised that students typically find difficult and disconcerting those tasks that require approaches other than set, formulaic written responses—tasks that ask them to engage material and respond thoughtfully. For the most part, they do not regularly perform such complex higher-order thought processes in situations that provide them with the guidance, feedback, and repetition they need to develop their ability to recognize changing contexts and then to react to them.

Yet that intellectual and communicative agility is an outcome expected of disciplinary study. Put simply, we expect students who finish a course of study (a class, a major, or a degree) to communicate the discipline's central tenets at something above novice proficiency. We want them to write like historians, mathematicians, physicists, or in my institution, pharmacists. And to write like a member of any given professional community, one must think like the majority of the community's practicing members. One must be able to sift through available information, analyze it and formulate appropriate questions and responses, and then evaluate this activity in a manner that allows drawing "legitimate" conclusions (Kuhn, 1970).

Traditional didactic classrooms offer students opportunities to carry out the initial information-gathering stages of this process. Students come away having been exposed to the core information and the data collection tools deemed appropriate by particular disciplinary communities. What they often do not acquire along the way, however, is the ability to step back from this body of information and evaluate it carefully and objectively. They have limited experience manipulating the evaluation tools used by their prospective professional community to undertake informed and accurate assessments of appropriateness, correctness, or merit of action and information. Ultimately, what grants disciplinary membership is not *what* one knows but *how* one goes about enlarging and testing that knowledge base.

If initiation into unique thought and communication systems is the implicit goal of most academic programs, it is interesting that students have few chances to develop the assessment skills that open the doors to disciplinary participation. Just as students need to be taught to access and process information in ways deemed acceptable by academic or professional disciplines, they should be explicitly taught to evaluate that same effort. While it is intellectually demanding to acquire the ability to step back and accurately and efficiently assess one's own performance, the good news is this: providing students with opportunities to learn the art of self-evaluation is not difficult.

Fitting Self-Evaluation Activities to Specific Contexts

Written self-assessments are applicable to and can be integrated into any course, with all students, and with most assignments. This claim may seem a bit heavy handed at first glance. However, working with teachers in disparate disciplines to incorporate writing in their content-based and often traditionally delivered courses, we repeatedly stumble on this truism: the success of any classroom activity is determined largely by the task's purpose. The same holds true for asking students to assess their own efforts and/or the efforts of their peers. If there is a demonstrable reason for asking students to engage seriously in the activity of written self-assessment, the basic groundwork exists for the activity's success.

What follows are two examples of very different courses that incorporate written self-evaluations in different ways for somewhat different purposes. In both courses, however, the justification for having students self-evaluate their performances are similar: the evaluations serve an essential role in teaching students to be more capable practitioners of quite different arts—pharmacy management and writing.

Case 1: Pharmacy Administration

Ken Schafermeyer, associate professor of pharmacy administration at St. Louis College of Pharmacy, teaches an introductory pharmacy management course with a typical enrollment of about 150. This large class size, combined with the physical limitations of the auditorium-style classroom and the extent of information covered, led Ken to doubt that he could incorporate any but the most rudimentary active learning strategies into the course. For several years, Think-Pair-Share and short question-answer sessions, for instance, helped pace the class sessions and provided opportunities for review of material. However, because his students are usually third-year students, Ken was particularly dismayed that many did not appear to learn from their mistakes on class assignments and exams—it seemed that they were not learning to think like managers who must be able to identify cause and effect relationships and prescribe remedies to deficient situations.

In reviewing the course, Dr. Schafermeyer and I discovered that in large part the only place students interacted with relevant management information in an attempt to apply it was in homework case studies sprinkled throughout the semester. These cases were designed to have students use analysis and synthesis skills to solve problems facing hypothetical pharmacy managers. Although the cases required students to pose multiple solutions and recommend specific courses of action, the main feedback that students received was more summative than formative: they were told whether or not their solutions were viable. With an average of 150 cases to review, Ken argued that providing extensive individual, formative feedback was unrealistic. Yet he believed that feedback would help students to perform more successfully on future cases.

Because Ken knew that his students had to develop their ability to self-assess their actions before they began to practice pharmacy, he added a two-question self-assessment activity (see Exhibit 4.1) to each homework case as a way to achieve two ends: (1) to give students multiple opportunities to practice using management evaluation tools in a meaningful context to evaluate their performance on specific tasks, and (2) to allow Ken a window into students' thinking processes, providing him with the information he needed to provide valuable feedback.

This activity asked students to assess their homework assignment by identifying its strengths and weaknesses. Following that, they were asked to explain in detail how they could improve their performance in the future. Although they were not asked overtly to explain *why* their assessments and strategies were valid, they had to provide this justification in order to deal effectively with the second question.

Upon receiving the homework with the self-assessment exercise attached, Ken skimmed the evaluations in order to compare students' solutions to their self-assessments and to see how well these correlated. Early on, students' self-evaluations fell into two extremes: hypercritical and overly optimistic. With

Exhibit 4.1. Case Study Self-Evaluation Instrument

PHARMACY MANAGEMENT
Financial Analysis Case Study

It has been said that "you learn by making mistakes." That's true, in a sense, because if you're not making mistakes, then you must not be trying new things. Conversely, a person could repeatedly make the same mistake without learning anything. Actually, a better way to say this is "you learn by recognizing and correcting your mistakes." The highest order of learning (and the most difficult) is evaluation. Good managers must be able to evaluate their own decisions and constantly try to improve upon them. That's why you are being asked to evaluate your own case study. Please do this evaluation by answering the following questions. Your score will be based on accuracy, completeness, and the proper use of terminology. Give this some thought before beginning to write. Please attach the copy of your "Case Report Form" to this sheet.

1. What did you do well in your analysis of the case? Be specific—give examples.

2. Assume that you are afforded the opportunity to do another financial analysis case study for a different pharmacy. Describe each of the steps listed on your "Case Report Form" that you feel you could improve on your next effort. Be specific—describe *what* you could improve and *how* you would do it.

practice, the students' assessments increased in accuracy and sophistication. Using this information, Ken looked for trends in the self-assessments as a basis for creating feedback designed to meet the problems that emerge as students deal with the problems situated in each case. Often this feedback includes overheads containing sample student self-assessments that illustrate a typical problem, take a unique approach, or are particularly well-argued. Doing so not only links Ken's responses concretely to specific examples, it also provides students with models of what evaluations at various levels of success and sophistication look like.

Case 2: First-Year Composition

Unlike most courses in the secondary or post-secondary curriculum, composition classes are more skills-based than content-based. This difference in focus readily predisposes composition classes to encouraging high levels of student active learning compared to many courses that are driven by the need to cover a specific content. Many writing classes employ mixtures of pairs and small and large groups, interspersed with student-teacher writing conferences as the principle class structure, with much of the activity centered around discovering and developing ideas and subsequent drafts of papers. These activities provide students with frequent opportunities to develop and practice analysis and synthesis skills. As part of the process of developing successful papers, however, writers need to evaluate their texts during development, and this is one area in which students need more instruction, modeling, and practice than they often receive.

Even in composition classes, students are sometimes more passive than active recipients of feedback. Although less frequently than in the past, many students receive a much larger measure of summative feedback than formative feedback. They are shown what is deficient or wrong with their texts, and often this feedback pays more attention to micro issues of grammatical or mechanical infelicities—items that are quite easy to mark—than to more global issues of rhetorical effectiveness or adequate levels of development that reflect students' thought processes—items that require extensive discussion.

Recognizing that by having to carefully critique their own papers my first-year composition students would gain needed experience in achieving critical distance from their own work, I introduced a series of self-evaluation activities to coincide with the submission of each paper. Although these activities are much more extensive than the evaluations Ken Schafermeyer uses in Pharmacy Management, they serve a similar purpose (see Exhibit 4.2). First, they give students multiple opportunities to practice analyzing and evaluating their own papers objectively; and second, they let me see the students' thinking processes and provide me with the information I need to give students timely, appropriate feedback.

First-year college students find the self-evaluation activities difficult at the start of the semester. The assignment is completed in one class period, and

Exhibit 4.2. Initial Self-Evaluation Instrument

Paper Critique

Today you are submitting an article for evaluation. Your assignment is to read your paper carefully and then to provide me with a written critique of the article. Because you are the author, you know more about the piece and about your writing than anyone. Therefore, please take the class period to complete the following assignment so I can benefit from your expertise.

I will use your critique as a road map to reading your article. It should allow me to find points of interest and miss tourist traps. Please include the following information:

What works well in the piece? Are there specific examples?
What would you like to change? Why?
Is there any place in the article that falls short? Why?
Who do you see as the article's intended audience?
How did you go about addressing that audience specifically?
How did you go about writing this piece?
Did this change since the last time you wrote a paper? Was it a change for the better?
What will you do differently next time? Why?
What one mechanical, grammatical, or structural problem would you like me to focus on when reading this article? Why?

This assignment may be more effective if you don't answer each question individually. Most of them work with others anyway. A memo or letter may be the best bet for an efficient way to get the information out.

although it provides specific questions for students to answer, in giving them wide latitude in presenting their assessment, the assignment throws many of them for a loop. For most students, this is the first time anyone has required them to assess their own writing. Instead of only receiving comments from the teacher in a top-down exercise of displaced authority, the authors themselves analyze and evaluate their texts. Additionally, they are also required to justify the validity of their assessment: they must demonstrate why the paper works as well as they claim it does, or why it does not.

This activity is designed to have writers carefully analyze the text they are submitting for evaluation, then synthesize the information that results into an assessment of the piece that evaluates its strengths and weaknesses. Successful writers eventually internalize this process to some extent; beginning and developing writers, however, at first need spread in front of them the tools appropriate for evaluating the success of written texts. The many *why* questions in the assignment's directions serve as these tools. With practice, students become more confident and more accurate in their self-assessments. As a result, as their plans to improve their future performance mature, the need for detailed and overly prescriptive commentary from me disappears. Most students are fully capable of pointing out the following: what works, and why; what does not, and why not; and what they can do about the situation, and why. Their critical accuracy lets me work one-to-one with students on issues unique to their writing, rather than addressing general comments to the entire class.

To provide a capstone experience, the final self-assessment for the course differs from the preceding ones by asking students to evaluate the final project against their efforts for the semester (see Exhibit 4.3). This assignment is challenging: it requires students to employ a much more complex frame of reference than any previous self-assessment activity, to evaluate more than one performance, and to perform the activity within strict time constraints. Invariably, students, having practiced this type of self-evaluation throughout the semester, are able to produce carefully reasoned and accurate assessments of their texts' strengths and weaknesses, as well as assess the strategies, decisions, and processes they employed to complete the text. These are evaluation skills that confident writers know how to employ to allow them to deal effectively and efficiently with new or unusual writing tasks. These skills are also an expected although frequently undertaught and underpracticed outcome for the composition course.

Planning for Written Self-Evaluation

The question one should ask when deciding whether or not to incorporate written self-evaluations into any course is this: How important is it for students in this course to be able to analyze and evaluate their work and then develop alternatives based on that reflection? If this skill is important to students' success in a course and to their assimilation into the community of professionals

Exhibit 4.3. Terminal Self-Evaluation Instrument

Paper #4: Critique

Because this is the last paper of the semester for this class, it should represent the culmination of your experience in this course. This paper should demonstrate your ability to use the strategies and skills you have further developed over the semester. In other words, this article should show me how much sharper your editorial ears and eyes have become since August.

In discussing the article you are submitting today for evaluation, I would like you to focus on two central questions:

1. What skill does this paper show convincingly that you have developed over the course of the semester? Demonstrate that development in comparison to the previous articles you have written for this course and explain why you identify this item as a major advancement for you.

2. What works particularly well in this article? Why? What decisions did you make during the writing of the article that helped to make this part of the article work as well as you claim it does?

Make sure that your critique also demonstrates your improved critical skills. In other words, support any claims you make with specific details that refer directly to the paper you are discussing. Get beyond generalities. Also, make sure you proofread the critique before you hand it in. You need to demonstrate that you can do this fairly well within a short amount of time.

represented by the course, a second question follows: What opportunities does the course currently offer students to learn and practice these evaluation skills with the feedback and repetition they need to increase their abilities to perform this higher-order critical activity? If the answer to this question is "few" or "none," activities modeled on those presented thus far may provide a foundation for helping students develop these skills.

Logistical Considerations

The issue of how to introduce written self-evaluation opportunities into courses prompts teachers to ask any number of questions as they plan for this type of classroom activity. Typically, the resulting questions can be grouped according to two prevalent themes: concerns for coverage and concerns for time constraints. Seeking to balance these concerns, you may find yourself asking, *What will have to go?* Very little, or as much as you wish. Most courses are packed to the gills with "necessary" information that needs to be transmitted to students. It can be difficult to see anywhere to make time for self-evaluation activities. Because written self-evaluations do not have to be either complicated or long, however, they can easily provide a needed pause in a lecture, giving students the opportunity to reflect on and assess assignments or material they may have prepared for the class period. It is remarkably easy, as the following example demonstrates, to provide students with opportunities to put developing self-evaluation skills to work without taking large chunks of time out of usually tight lecture schedules.

Ken Schafermeyer uses self-evaluation questions at the start of the period (three to five minutes) to allow students to reassess their homework before class discussion. Answering simple questions such as *What do you see as the weak/strong link in your response to the homework problem? and Why?* encourages students to concretely link their out-of-class preparation to class activities. When students review and analyze their preparatory efforts, they are more readily able to formulate cogent questions and articulate concerns at a level of specificity that makes the ensuing class lectures and discussions more productive. Their self-assessments—which Ken often collects as a roll-taking mechanism—often show that although the students can chug the management data provided through appropriate data-analysis formulas, they can have difficulties grasping the overarching concepts that explain and drive the formulas they use. With this information, Ken can alter the next class period's agenda to help meet students' needs as they present themselves, rather than when he anticipates they will arise.

Following closely on the heels of questions about what to give up in order to include written student self-evaluations is the question, *How much, how soon?* Start slowly. Too often teachers think that unless they go all out with a new idea or classroom approach, they are not doing enough. This all-or-nothing approach can be disastrous. You must consider both your and your students' comfort levels with the activity.

As the person responsible for the overall success of the course, you should never commit yourself to any activity with which you are not completely comfortable. In many classes—particularly core and introductory lecture courses—adding student self-assessment writing assignments is quite alien. Not only is extensive writing not traditionally part of these courses, but they tend to target students early in their educational experience—students who initially may not successfully perform such demanding critical tasks as those implicit in writing carefully considered self-evaluations. Both of these issues are very real and understandable, and thus can contribute to making many teachers uneasy about introducing such tasks.

My writing courses are now structured almost entirely around student self-evaluations. That structure, however, did not happen overnight. Instead, I have developed and added these types of activities for many years; as my understanding has increased I have modified the courses as to what written self-assessment activities can accomplish and what types of self-evaluation skills students need to develop and practice. My first efforts were extremely rudimentary, yet the positive outcomes they produced encouraged me to continue experimenting and expanding.

Admittedly, success in using written student self-evaluations is never guaranteed. This lack of certainty gives rise to the final question, *What if it does not work?* Do not fret. First, keep going, then take some time to analyze the situation carefully and evaluate your performance. You may find that you are not at fault. It may just have been one of those days: the fire alarms in the dorms may have gone off all night long; everyone's biorhythms may be off. As with any classroom activity—even lectures—one should always have a backup plan to employ when planned activities do not come off as originally envisioned. I often use these instances to engage students in more metacognitive activity. Instead of abandoning a "failed" written self-assessment activity altogether, I ask students to analyze and evaluate it as a text that does not accomplish its designed purpose, and to suggest alternatives that might allow it to work more effectively. The prompt I keep just offstage for such situations looks like this: This activity did not accomplish its intended purpose. Look it over carefully and suggest how it could be recast more effectively. What does your alternative offer that the original did not?

Assorted Tips and Advice

Some courses are more immediately amenable to written self-evaluations than others. This fact acknowledged, however, any course—regardless of disciplinary affiliation or content-coverage issues—can use this active learning activity successfully. While writing courses lend themselves immediately to self-evaluation activities based in writing, at my institution teachers of such disparate courses as organic chemistry, calculus, physics, and current issues in infectious diseases have successfully and consistently integrated written self-evaluation into their courses as one more means of achieving specific course outcomes.

Keep tinkering with the activities. Like fine wine and fresh bread, any written self-assessment activity can go flat and stale. Usually, this results from the fact that the activity was not designed specifically to accompany the task it is linked to—the activity is out of context or too repetitive. Repetition is a useful learning algorithm; however, rote is boring and sends the contradictory message that both the original task and the assessment activity are not truly important. It does not take much time to retool a standard self-assessment activity to fit a specific task, and the time is well spent.

Always add the tag question: Why? The toughest part of crafting students' written self-assessment activities is getting the questions to illicit the type of response desired. I almost always revise these questions several times before I try them out on student audiences, yet when the activities don't perform as I expect, I invariably find that the questions were worded such that students could answer them in a closed-ended manner. Finding a yes or a no answer to what I consider a finely crafted prompt is always startling. Almost always the remedy is simple: add the tag question *why.* Tag questions keep prompts open-ended, encouraging students to dig deeper into their analysis to produce an adequate justification of their position.

Provide some type of consistent feedback early on. Because students are almost always hesitant to commit fully to unfamiliar activities, they need to be reassured that their initial attempts are valid. Feedback is essential if they are to develop the trust in you and in the process of publicly evaluating their efforts that they need to hone their self-assessment skills (Beaven, 1977). This feedback does not have to be extensive, however, nor does it have to come only from you, the teacher.

Although I recommend that on a first attempt every student receive some feedback—even an "I agree" in the margin by one accurate observation—on subsequent assessments half or less of the class can receive your comments. By responding to every other or every third assessment, not only will every student receive personalized feedback, but you will not have to spend an inordinate amount of time on this task. Additionally, selective sampling of the available responses affords you the opportunity to choose model self-assessments for discussion in the class and to address common issues.

Students can also receive feedback from their peers. In fact, often peer critique is more effective than teacher generated feedback because students often need greater levels of acceptance and praise from peers than they need from teachers. An additional benefit of peer feedback comes from the fact that this activity takes the task of evaluation one step further, keeping students actively engaged in evaluation on two simultaneous fronts—their partner's text and, often unknowingly, their own.

Keep letter grades out of it when possible. This tip is a logical extension of the previous one: feedback, not grades, is the important outcome with self-assessment because encouraging continued intellectual growth and critical abilities is the central goal of these activities. I find that students will write thoughtful and accurate self-evaluations when this activity receives points that figure very little in the overall course grade. When vying for an A, B, or C, students often resort to trying to psych out the teacher and give me what they think I want, rather than assessing their performance objectively. I find it useful to mark self-assessments using the following scale:

√ - (appeared to put little thought into the activity)
√ (engaged the questions, but response needs more support/explanation)
√ + (good-faith-to-excellent effort; position supported with details)

At the end of the semester I tally these scores against the number of opportunities students had to self-evaluate. The resulting percentage accounts for between 10 and 15 percent of the course grade. This keeps the grading element out of the students' experience during the semester.

Final Thoughts

Although written student self-assessments often seem exotic at first glance, they are anything but. All they are is a pragmatic response to a nagging problem: how to create situations that allow students to learn to step back from their work and evaluate it productively. Written self-assessments offer much more than other available types of student self-assessment mechanisms, particularly Likert-scale-type assessment questionnaires. While they are easy to score, Likert scale assessment questionnaires provide little information that is student specific. Instead, they generate pictures of general patterns across a large number of students.

More problematic is the fact that these type of self-assessments require students to engage in the act of evaluation only briefly. They are not asked to analyze their responses and provide any support for their judgements. That failure highlights the strengths of written self-assessments. Not only do these questions require students to engage them for longer periods of time and, hopefully, at more concerted levels of thought, they also provide students with opportunities to practice higher-order critical skills for meaningful purposes—to create options by which they may improve their performance in the future.

If the purpose of most classes is to help students enter into a community of like-minded persons—nurses, philosophers, accountants, or pharmacy managers—then their course activities should facilitate that entrance. To make that entrance, students must be able to think, make decisions, and evaluate their actions using the same tools as other members of that community. To do so successfully, students need instruction in how these activities are undertaken, and opportunities to practice and to receive formative feedback about their efforts to put these skills into play.

In providing an environment that supports this type of development, we create the space students need to learn how to think about their thinking. These metacognitive skills are the tools that enable students to learn in the many different and often ambiguous situations in which they will find themselves as members of a professional community. The ability to actively engage one's actions and objectively assess them with the purpose of developing alternatives is the key to independent, lifelong learning. These skills are course and institutional outcomes worth striving to help students realize.

Afterword

Much of the material presented in this chapter has come directly from classes that I and my colleagues have taught, and as such is somewhat idiosyncratic. These activities are, however, not without precedent or variation. This exploration of student written self-evaluation as an active learning strategy owes much to Donald Murray's collection *Learning By Teaching* (1982), particularly his essay "The Listening Eye: Reflections of the Writing Conference." I have presented a more detailed discussion of the first critique of student papers activity in "Student Evaluations Do More Than Ease Grading Loads" (Hobson, 1991), and the essays in Camposella's (1993) earlier-mentioned collection also provide fruitful discussions focusing more on writing and evaluation as critical thinking. Finally, a growing body of work in the teacher-training literature has been looking at the benefits of using journals with student teachers as a means of developing self-evaluation.

References

Beaven, M. H. "Individualized Goal Setting, Self-Evaluation, and Peer Evaluation." In C. R. Cooper and L. Odell (eds.), *Evaluating Writing: Describing, Measuring, Judging.* Urbana, Ill.: National Council of Teachers of Education, 1977.

Bloom, B. S. (ed.). *Taxonomy of Educational Objectives: The Classification of Educational Goals.* New York: Longman, 1956.

Bonwell, C. C., and Eison, J. A. *Active Learning: Creating Excitement in the Classroom.* ASHE-ERIC Higher Education Report No. 1. Washington D.C.: George Washington University, School of Education and Human Development, 1991.

Camposella, T. L. (ed.). *The Critical Writing Workshop: Designing Assignments to Foster Critical Thinking.* Portsmouth, N.H.: Boynton/Cook, 1993.

Dewey, J. *Education and Experience.* Old Tappan, N.J.: Macmillan, 1963.

Hobson, E. "Student Evaluations Do More Than Ease Grading Loads." *Tennessee English Journal,* 1991, 2, 20–22.

Kuhn, T. S. *The Structure of Scientific Revolutions* (2nd ed.). Chicago: University of Chicago Press, 1970.

Matsuhashi, A. "Pausing and Planning: The Tempo of Written Discourse Production." *Research in the Teaching of English,* 1981, 15, 113–134.

Murray, D. *Learning by Teaching.* Portsmouth, N. H.: Boynton/Cook, 1982.

Vygotsky, L. S. *Thought and Language* (E. Hanfmann and G. Vakar, trans.). Cambridge, Mass: MIT Press, 1962.

Young, A., and Fulwiler, T. (eds.). *Writing Across the Disciplines: Research into Practice.* Portsmouth, N. H.: Boynton/Cook, 1986.

ERIC H. HOBSON *directs the Writing Center and coordinates the Writing Program at St. Louis College of Pharmacy. He is coauthor of* Reading and Writing in High Schools: A Whole Language Approach *(National Education Association, 1990), and has published widely on issues surrounding ways to provide support systems for student writers.*

Electronic media provide faculty with new opportunities for designing strategies to engage students both in and out of the classroom.

Using Electronic Tools to Promote Active Learning

David H. Gillette

"Hi. I had a question in class about the last chapter on Tuesday but was embarrassed to ask it because I thought it might sound kind of stupid. And that I should have picked up the answer by just reading the chapter. Well, I didn't come up with the answer and I'm afraid if I don't ask I'll get behind. I don't quite understand. . . ."

Most professors at least suspect that questions like this go unanswered each semester, if not each week or each class period. This question, received on electronic-mail (e-mail) shortly after class ended that day, did not. It was asked and answered within hours following a class the student had prepared for but remained confused about after attending. The question was in fact not stupid but rather dealt with a fundamental building block that is frequently misunderstood and can be a source of faulty reasoning throughout the semester. E-mail provided this student with rapid access to the professor even though neither person could have met with the other that afternoon. For this student the learning process continued, that is, remained alive and active, even though personal inhibitions precluded open participation in the classroom.

As its name implies, e-mail allows people to send and receive mail electronically using computers just as they would send paper mail with envelopes and stamps using the postal service—except that it happens virtually instantaneously, and without paper, envelopes, or stamps. Once logged on to their

The author extends sincere appreciation to faculty members on his campus whose experience and insights contributed to the development, compilation, and quality of this chapter. Special thanks to Anne Ellsworth, Paula Cochran, Karen Hirsch, Shirley Morahan, and Steve Reschley.

institution's computing facilities, users can create and send mail anytime it is convenient. Mail arrives almost immediately within the same computing system, and literally within seconds when mail is sent across the country over the Internet. After arriving, e-mail waits in a file (the recipient's "mailbox") until the person wishes to read it. The process of sending e-mail is usually menu driven, and most computer systems notify the user when they log onto the computer that mail has arrived.

Another mechanism for electronic communication, electronic conferencing, resembles a sophisticated form of graffiti, with the exceptions that there is no wall, the topics are more wholesome and edifying, and the contributors are usually identified at least by their computer identification number. Conference discussions typically center around a specific topic, event, or activity in an ongoing file maintained by the mainframe computer, where comments from each conference participant are dated and stored for later access by other conference members. Conference participants both view and post comments at their personal convenience. Electronic conferences have the attractive feature that access to them can be open to the public or restricted to a limited group of participants such as the members of a specific course or organization.

A worldwide network of networks, the Internet, first began in the U.S. defense industry to connect researchers with each other. It was then expanded by the National Science Foundation to include additional research facilities both in the United States and around the world, and has since grown to link millions of computers globally. Formally, the Internet is a system of software standards, called protocols, that allow all different types of computers and local area networks to communicate with each other over telephone lines in a standardized format. In practice, the Internet remains transparent to the user except that communication takes place between sites around the world, literally within a flash. Unlike e-mail however, by which messages are simply sent and wait to be read, Internet users actually connect to other computer systems and interact with them as if they were on location with the system to which they are connected. On most campuses the World Wide Web has become an additional means for accessing electronic information. A unique aspect of "the Web" is the inclusion of multimedia elements as well as text. It is possible to access pictures, graphics, even movies within the web environment. Navigation of the Web requires the use of a "browser" such as Netscape, Mosaic, or Lynx, all of which are programs that use the Internet to find and retrieve Web documents located on various computers around the world.

Electronic media provide teaching professors with several advantages ranging from increased instructor availability through e-mail to class discussions that extend "beyond the bell," through conferencing to worldwide classrooms through the Internet and the Web. These benefits, however, are not without cost to the instructor, nor do they meet with universal acceptance by students asked to participate in them. This chapter provides a broad overview of the contributions electronic media can make to active learning. It also provides guidance to minimizing the costs of including them and maximizing student enthusiasm for these kinds of course activities. The primary focus will be on e-mail, with secondary emphasis on conferencing and some limited discussion of the Internet. Treatment will remain general in nature and free of specific hardware and software configurations, which are best explored through local computer services centers.

Low levels of computer sophistication should warrant neither alarm nor panic from instructors interested in incorporating these tools in their courses. No matter how awkward or inexperienced instructors may feel using electronic media, the examples and suggestions contained in this chapter should serve as springboards to computer-assisted activities that are capable of providing faculty with a greater variety of active learning practices for their courses. Courage and the desire for students to take greater charge of their own learning make up the primary prerequisites for those interested in these tools. Readers wishing to explore additional sources should consult the suggestions for further reading given at the end of this chapter.

As with each of the pedagogical tools discussed in this book, computers should not be viewed as the solution to every classroom challenge or teaching goal an instructor might encounter or strive for. Ideally, computers and electronic media should serve as one of several tools available. Each teaching opportunity can likely be approached with any one or more of these tools. With careful planning and good fortune each tool should help generate additional, even spontaneous, teaching opportunities that individual instructors can utilize to facilitate an active, responsive teaching and learning environment. E-mail, the basic building block for both conferencing and the Internet, serves well in this context as a model for discussing various issues involved in developing an electronically assisted classroom.

Uses and Examples from Practice

"I never went to visit him. If I had trouble, I wrote him on e-mail."
"He talked to me during office hours, after class, walking on campus, through e-mail. All talks with him were helpful."
"I never visited but I did e-mail him and I received quick and helpful responses."

Such were representative responses from one instructor's course evaluations when students were asked if visits outside the classroom and during regular office hours were helpful. (No mention of e-mail was made in the prompt.) So began that instructor's use of electronic media as a course component. Beginning with e-mail, the uses for electronic media seem limited only by an instructor's own imagination and creativity. The collection of possibilities provided here reflects only a few of the tested favorites in use on my campus.

E-Mail. First-day assignments on e-mail can be used both to familiarize students with the computing facilities and just to have a little fun. Some instructors assign students to submit a letter of self-introduction through e-mail. Or they ask students to send a one- or two-sentence e-mail message describing their impressions of the first day of class; in this way an instructor can gather quite a bit of valuable information. For example, one student wrote, "The first day of class I learned how to use the e-mail system and most importantly that I could actually get along with upper classmen." Another wrote, "Hello. My first day of class was very interesting. My immediate impression was one of surprise and bewilderment. I expected to hear an hour and a half of boring lecture and notes, instead I got you." It is important that these exercises be clearly defined, adequately supported, and nonthreatening.

Daily use of e-mail has been successfully combined with a one-minute writing exercise. Students write one or two sentences on a scrap of paper about the most important thing (MIT) they learned that day and turn it in as they leave class. All of the MITs are compiled anonymously into one file, either by a student worker or by the instructor. The file is then transferred to the mainframe and distributed to each member of the class using an electronic mailing list, a standard feature on most mailing facilities. (This sounds like quite a process, but once the file is created it can be transferred and the mail sent to the whole class in three to five minutes.) Generally most of the main points of that day's discussion will be mentioned, and the instructor not only receives immediate feedback about what students got out of class that day but can also, if desired, quickly edit the comments for accuracy (course-related accuracy only, to inhibit misunderstanding of key principles), allowing students to use the comments as a check and review of that day's coverage.

Many students comment about the usefulness of the MITs as a course component. One wrote that "the MITs helped a great deal, to give us something to think about as we left class." Another commented, "I do learn from the entries of other students. I have copied some of the entries that helped 'sum up' what we learned in class that particular day to help me study that night." Yet another student's e-mail message exemplified some of the candor students feel comfortable displaying: "I think that the MITs are a good thing, but I don't like the ones that say stuff like, 'I should read more.' I think they should be a fact about economics. They do help me review after the class is over, but only the ones that actually say something about the class discussion."

Another example of such candor took place between an economics instructor and one of his more shy students as they sent several messages back and forth discussing the "economics" of one partner having sex with the other in order to "appease" or "to be exempt from harassment." After the instructor's final response, the student sent another message thanking him for his time and for helping to "really clear things up." The student's most relevant statement, for this context, came in her first message when she asked that the instructor respond "over e-mail [since she was] not really sure if [she] could handle a classroom discussion of this nature . . . [but found this] brutally interesting." Throughout the remainder of the semester they continued to have stimulating e-mail exchanges and developed a rapport. But she never did volunteer to make in-class contributions in front of other students.

Distribution of any number or type of textual items can also be accomplished by e-mail. For example, class discussion will frequently generate an issue or a question that deserves a more thoughtful or thought out response than can be given on the spur of the moment or than class time allows. Or the instructor simply might not know the answer. E-mail serves as a useful mechanism on such occasions, when responding before the next class period seems appropriate. It also allows distribution of critical information, such as a necessary clarification or an addendum to a homework assignment that is discovered only as it is passed out in class. In such instances the instructor can easily compile the necessary materials, transfer them to the mainframe, and send them to each student in the class within hours of the end of class. An instructor might also wish to distribute scanned-in news articles or offer extra credit opportunities using e-mail. Midterm evaluations in the form of a few sentences about what is or is not working for each student are also a useful form of feedback. Students generally do appreciate the opportunity to voice their opinions while there is a chance for changes to be made. Another particularly informative e-mail exercise is to have students mail the instructor two or three sentences about their impressions of and performance on an exam before it is returned to them in class.

As indicated earlier, e-mail also provides additional opportunities for instructors and students to interact with each other through "electronic" office hours. Though possibly not immediately, students using e-mail have the advantage of one-on-one attention from their instructor. A frequently raised question regarding such interaction concerns students e-mail demeanor. Wide experience across several disciplines suggests that the distance provided by the electronic medium allows a significant portion of students to actually open up much more using e-mail than they do either in class or during an office visit. This experience occurs not only between students and the instructor using e-mail but also between class members when a class conferences over the course of a whole semester (Bump, 1990; Cooper and Selfe, 1990).

Conferencing.   Conferencing and e-mail have the common characteristic that they occur outside the classroom. Both engage students directly with a different kind of commitment of time and effort than an assignment of "Go home and read Chapter Two," which some will read word for word, some will skim, and some will not read at all. Depending on the extent of the conferences available to the class, electronic conferencing adds another dimension of activity. Students become "active choosers" as they decide what to read and what to disregard. They also become "active investors" because e-mail and conferencing yield greater returns the more students invest in them. Electronic conferences allow students to leave class knowing they can still voice their views even though there was not enough time during the class period. They also give more students than just those with the tendency to speak up in class the ability to participate in the discussion and to help set the agenda for what that discussion should be about.

Uses for electronic conferences seem limitless. Classes meeting only once a week use them to sustain on-going conversation throughout the semester.

Instructors using modems can visit and supervise student internships, field work, and clinical settings at remote sites while continuing to communicate with class members between weekly meetings. Successful conferences have been conducted in disciplines across the curriculum including African-American issues, biology, communication disorders, economics, education, English, environmental issues, history, psychology, Spanish, theater, world cinema, and world literature. Typically, conferences allow a class to carry on a reflective discussion about a significant topic without the constraints of the period ending in a few minutes while there is still a mass of critical material left to cover. Variations on this theme include a children's literature class in which students collectively read literally hundreds of books during a semester. In this class each student works on an individual project and looks for particular books for particular purposes. The electronic conference in this course serves a secondary function of a registry for electronic want ads. Students post not only comments about books they are reading but also comments about books they have been unable to locate and about the kinds of books they would still like to search out. The conference serves as a convenient bulletin board where members of the class can make and respond to such wishes without having to track someone down, catch someone on the phone, or rely on everyone having an answering machine on which dozens of messages can be left.

The Internet. The contexts described so far have involved usage of only local university computing facilities. Another dimension of using electronic media extends beyond the local environment to all of the facilities available through a worldwide system of linked computer networks, the Internet. Examples of incorporating student communication with other sites include pairing of the same classes on different campuses in a conference in which both classes discuss the same topics together. Students' exposure to a broader, often more diverse group of discussants provides additional insights and learning experiences, frequently including the validation that they are not "the only ones required to learn this stuff." In the case of one women's history class, students were required to sign on to a list server discussion group or bulletin board that in some way dealt with women's history issues. Having students encounter people on the Internet with real-life experiences similar to those discussed in class legitimated a whole set of topics and concerns that otherwise had not been taken less seriously in the past. The Web is a resource for finding information on virtually any topic.

Planning to Use These Tools

"Thanks for an hour of racking my brain in microchip hell. I had to use about five computers before I finally got anywhere, but the pleasure of accomplishment was worth it."

"I learned . . . how to use e-mail, except it didn't quite look the same or as easy as you made it seem."

"Although I have never before worked with e-mail or used computers for any purpose save word processing, I like what I have seen. I sincerely hope that many of our assignments can be turned in electronically, like this."
"I have learned how to use e-mail after being here for two years. It is so easy, but I never took the time to learn."

After the first day of class, when students discover the e-mail component of the course and receive their first assignment, experiences getting acquainted with e-mail vary greatly depending on the students' computer background. The above comments represent the type and range of experiences students have, even with a relatively thorough introduction to using e-mail. Several things can affect the degree of success an instructor and class will experience using electronic media to communicate with each other during the semester. They are discussed here in a somewhat logical sequence, but not necessarily in order of importance. In preparation for writing this chapter, faculty at Truman State University (formerly Northeast Missouri State University, prior to July 1, 1996) who have experience using electronic tools in their classes were interviewed. Many of their experiences and suggestions have been incorporated in this section and throughout this chapter.

Achievement of Course Objectives. An instructor's objective for incorporating electronic communication must receive paramount consideration and cannot be ignored. The use of e-mail, conferencing, or the Internet should not be incorporated in a course just to make the claim that technology is being used, but only when an instructor seriously wants to open lines of communication to a broader cross section of students or to pursue some topics in more depth over a longer period of time. Nor may an instructor just assign these activities and expect students to complete them successfully on their own. An implicit theme of this chapter is the suggestion that course objectives related to electronic media will remain unrealized if an instructor only administrators the course instead of actively participating in the learning and communication process.

Level of Computer Sophistication. Computer literacy on the part of both instructors and students frequently heads the list of concerns raised by those contemplating the use of electronic media in a class. Instructors and students come with all levels of proclivity and resistance towards using computers. Some will hate them. Some will love them. Most hatred towards computers by those who have used them can be traced to a bad initial experience. And although only a nominal level of computer literacy on the part of the student is required to use e-mail and electronic conferencing, lack of a minimum level of computer competency on the part of the instructor can and probably will turn the initial experience for most students, and for the instructor, into a bad one. In general the best advice is to plan well and not try to pull off these types of activities on the spur of the moment.

Time Commitment. Earlier mention acknowledged that the benefits of e-mail and conferencing do not come without cost, nor do most worthwhile activities. Start-up costs in terms of time can be substantial but will vary among instructors, depending on their level of computer background and on the user friendliness of their particular institution's computing facilities. Once the initial time costs of learning how to use the resident computing system have been paid, a significant time commitment, depending on class size and instructor dedication, will still be required. E-mail messages and conference contributions must both be read and responded to since students' acceptance and enthusiasm for these activities wanes quickly when they feel that their work disappears into an electronic black hole. Frankly, instructors who want to spend less than sixty minutes of preparation per fifty-minute class period should probably avoid these teaching tools.

Conversely, instructors who continue to use these techniques claim that the benefits in terms of course enrichment and professor-student rapport far outweigh the time costs involved, and they become more efficient using these tools. Depending on the size of the class and the extent of use, time commitments can range from less than an hour to several hours a week. If simply responding to an established e-mail assignment from a class, it may be possible to spend only an hour or so. If preparing directions and procedures for a new activity and responding to students' initial attempts, several hours might be consumed in a week. Faculty who use these approaches report that the significant time commitment required to use them are balanced by the flexibility of when and where the instructor's involvement occurs. Given the flexibility that home computers, laptops, and modems provide, the time spent by instructors on these activities does not have to coincide with a student's presence in their office. For example, when necessary, one instructor in education maintains daily contact with her students on campus while visiting student interns across the state. Many instructors also argue that the time spent per student on electronic communication averages far less than the time spent per student on live office visits. While there are clear benefits to using electronic tools in teaching, the amount of time required by these activities should not be underestimated. Nor should the role of time commitment on the part of students be underestimated. Students must make time to learn about the process, access the mainframe or an otherwise networked computer, and participate in what often becomes an additional activity required of them by instructors. In compensation, some instructors feel justified factoring in the cancellation of a class period and making that additional time available to students. Other instructors cut back on what they feel might, under the circumstances, be less critical course components, while still others simply resort to requiring students to participate by allocating some portion of the course grade to a "conference" component. And yes, extra credit works too.

Class Size. While contributing directly to the time commitment required to maintain these activities over the course of a semester, class size should not become a deterrent but rather should be a factor to consider when planning the extent to which an instructor employs electronic communication as a course component. Smaller classes, with fewer than thirty students, seem optimal in terms of following through with the greatest levels of involvement.

However, with reasonable modifications successful experiences have occurred in classes with sixty, eighty, and even two hundred students (McClelland, 1993). As with any writing assignment, larger classes mean that fewer pages per student can be read over the course of a semester, and to the extent that students take it seriously, an instructor will spend more time answering e-mail with two hundred and fifty students in a class than with twenty-five. While instructors might consider reducing their expectations in terms of the number of contributions each student will make to an electronic conference, they will probably not want to quell the excitement that would generate more frequent voluntary contributions. Internet assignments could then be treated similarly, in terms of frequency and magnitude, to other types of homework assignments that would normally be assigned in a larger class environment. As indicated earlier, an instructor should recognize that choosing to use these methods will require a certain commitment of time, and choosing to use them in larger classes will require more time if they are employed to the same degree as in a smaller class. Nonetheless, many instructors argue that for them the benefits have weighed in more heavily than the costs.

Course Structure. An important issue implicit throughout this chapter pertains to the level of structure necessary to successfully incorporate these uses of technology. Although that level varies among e-mail, conferencing, and the Internet, more structure is usually required than seems apparent from the perspective of a naive observer, and more structure is always required relative to a comparable course without an electronic communications component. Plan on planning; these tools may be self-perpetuating, but they are not self-generating. An instructor can always jettison a certain activity or component of a course outline in a pinch, or in a disaster, but impromptu implementation of these tools generally results in one of those bad experiences that sours students' enthusiasm for working in a computing environment.

Technical Difficulties. As the first quote in this section, about "microchip hell," indicates, not all computers are created equal. Nor will instructors beginning to experiment with these forms of electronic communication always feel adequately prepared to explore the electronic universe that awaits them. Besides making new friends in computer services, colleagues who use e-mail and conferences are excellent resources to be aware of and are generally quite willing to be of assistance. Normally there will be little an instructor can do about hardware problems, but knowing the difference between hardware problems and software quirks can take the sting out of otherwise bad experiences. Learn flexibility and spontaneous creativity. Fortunately the world has yet to end because of a computer failure.

When using electronic tools in class, an instructor's greatest fear might be the effect that computer difficulties would have on the classroom environment when something goes wrong just minutes before or after class begins. How can that experience be made up for? Can that allotment of time just go to waste? A little anticipation, ingenuity, and perseverance will prevail. Develop contingency plans for the event of computer downtime (which always occur when it is least convenient) and go on with life. Some of the most memorable class-room experiences begin with disaster, particularly if the instructor prepares for it. These situations are similar to having a blown overhead projector bulb—the instructor is left standing with a handful of overhead transparencies and no place to display them. Instructors should not become dependent on these or any other teaching tools to the extent that their course cannot go on with-out them. Let the tools serve to enhance the quality of the learning environ-ment rather than function as a taskmaster whom the instructor or the students must serve.

Computers seldom "go down" for more than a few hours and almost never for more than a day or two. In general, students are quite flexible and will survive quite well on those rare occasions when they have to wait a few hours to send or receive an e-mail message or to participate in an electronic conference. They will also recover quite deftly from postponing by one class period an in-class activity involving e-mail, conference, or Internet particulars. Each instructor will end up resolving little "emergencies" differently, and per-haps even differently for different courses, but anyone using these tools should plan for something to go wrong sometime, take it in good spirits, and make the best of it.

Students, however, will become frustrated if they keep having to redis-cover each system quirk for themselves. Keeping a log of the questions and problems encountered or reported to the instructor and making students aware of them and of their solutions will go a long way towards eliminating any frus-trations created by the use of computer technology. Some instructors choose to develop extensive handouts to guide students through each type of com-puter usage expected of them and to cover each of the foreseen questions and problems students could encounter. Handouts can either be distributed to each student along with the easy-to-follow instructions or made available if and when problems are encountered. Other instructors find it quite useful to sim-ply schedule an early class period in a computer lab where everyone receives hands-on practice doing what will be expected of them. Still other instructors find it more appropriate to schedule an evening workshop or two for only those students unfamiliar with using the computing facilities. Depending on the computer support services on each campus, these sessions could be con-ducted either by the instructor or by a campus computer consultant.

Simple, Easy-to-Follow Instructions. E-mail, conferencing, the Web, and the Internet will present a challenge to at least some students in any class. For those least precocious in the world of computers, even a simple task such as logging onto a mainframe may seem intimidating. Nothing will discourage students more rapidly from using e-mail or signing onto a conference than a bad first experience. As mentioned earlier, making the first experience a good one will in most cases require significant personal preparation on the part of instructors. They must understand and be prepared to teach the use of the technology they want students to use. Instructors who keep track of problems and questions encountered while developing their computer activities, and who prepare a brief handout of instructions, along with pitfalls to avoid, will encounter far less resistance and much more success incorporating computers into their course environment. Using computers to communicate with students outside the classroom will then enhance rather than detract from the quality of the course. Keeping track of the problems students encounter during the first semester or two facilitates revisions to the handout that will empower most students to solve problems on their own. Any problem the instructor has ever had or even heard about should be a candidate for inclusion. Such a handout accompanied by an introductory, foolproof assignment designed to familiarize and give students confidence in using the computer normally provides a good first experience and creates a positive atmosphere for the remainder of the course. Instructors serious about creating a positive computing environment find that students are enthusiastic about a class period or extra orientation session held during the first week or two of the semester to get them up to speed on the computing skills they will need.

Privacy Issues. Since in many computer systems each user's identification number or nickname accompanies any comments posted on e-mail or to an electronic conference, a frequent concern of instructors is that students will hold back controversial comments out of concern over peer reaction. Overwhelming experience suggests that instructors' concerns about nonanonymous contributions inhibiting students' openness and sincerity seem unwarranted. Instructors here at Truman have noticed little if any reluctance due to the lack of anonymity on the part of students to put forth their comments. Some computer systems do, however, allow users to suppress their identity; instructors should consult with computer services at their individual institutions about their system's capabilities. If students unable to contribute anonymously have concerns about the impact of controversial messages, instructors can encourage them to first try posting a less controversial message and check out the effect it causes. In any event, all users of any public or private electronic medium should be encouraged to adhere to proper and acceptable etiquette while a guest of the system they are using.

Strolling Through the Electronic Universe. The ever-present risk of whiling away many hours when using electronic communication media plays no favorites among students or instructors. Only a few minutes dabbling on the Web reveal nearly unlimited options for browsing interesting sites around the world (Falk, 1994). Many people find e-mailing a lot of fun, preferable in many ways to regular letter writing, homework, research, or lecture preparation. Both students and instructors find a plethora of other activities in which they can participate. And before long they can easily spend hours meandering through the Internet. However, all this cost need not be void of redeeming qualities; meanderers become exposed to, and perhaps interested in, relevant material of which they would otherwise remain unaware. The discovery of such material through voluntary, individual pursuit of further knowledge illustrates at least one type of the "active learning" we are trying to engender.

Other Issues

Imagine a continuum of student involvement with straight lecture and note taking at the left and total interaction with no room for note taking at the right. E-mail and conferencing might on the surface appear to fall more towards the left on such a continuum. Experienced instructors judge that even in more formal, straight-lecture settings students' involvement with course material rises with this additional engagement outside the classroom.

One instructor commented that students can often use conference discussions as a resource for writing papers or studying for tests. When used as a resource for writing papers, an as yet unresolved issue requiring further consideration involves the citing of material found in conferences or elsewhere on the Internet. This issue becomes even more relevant when students are expected by their instructors to pursue and incorporate material they have found on the Internet into formal writing assignments. Be prepared to state your preferences, or give students direction to an appropriate manual of style.

Even as this book goes to press, new frontiers await exploration. One of the Internet features is a tool called Gopher, which through a system of hierarchical menus lets the user explore and retrieve information from various databases across the nation and around the world. Developed by the University of Minnesota, Gopher has been around for quite some time by computing standards. The newest frontier, the World Wide Web, is a hypertext interface to many of the same and other resources available through the Internet. Access to the Web with a browsing tool is similar to Gopher except that the user must have a graphics capability to receive the visuals in the transmission. Links to other documents in the Web are more lateral than hierarchical and are achieved by clicking a mouse on textual menu items. Although the Web is a fairly new phenomenon, faculty on many campuses are already using it as a teaching tool for themselves and a learning tool for their students. Readers are encouraged to be aware of this opening frontier and pursue its exploration as the Web becomes available to more and more institutions across the nation.

References

Bump, J. "Radical Changes in Class Discussion Using Networked Computers." *Computers in the Humanities*, 1990, *24*, 49–65.

Cooper, M. M., and Selfe, C. L. "Computer Conferences and Learning: Authority, Resistance, and Internally Persuasive Discourse." *College English*, 1990, *52*, 847–869.

Falk, B. *The Internet Roadmap*. Alameda, Calif.: Sybex, 1994.

McClelland, A. "E-Mailing a Large Class." *IT Times*, 1993, *1* (5). Davis: The Information Technology Division, University of California, Davis.

DAVID H. GILLETTE *is an associate professor of economics at Truman State University (formerly known as Northeast Missouri State University).*

Students working cooperatively in carefully-structured small groups can maximize their own and each other's learning.

Cooperative Learning: Making "Groupwork" Work

Karl A. Smith

When students attend a college class, they typically expect to sit passively and listen to a professor "profess"; they expect to be evaluated based on their individual work—exams, papers, and quizzes—and they bring with them a set of norms for interacting with their classmates. Based on their past experiences with school, many students believe that they are in competition with their classmates for scarce resources—good grades. Even when faculty use a performance-based or absolute grading system, students may recognize that they are not in competition with their classmates, but they may only vaguely sense that their classmates' grades are unrelated to theirs. Competitive interaction among students and no interaction among students (individualistic evaluation) are the two most common ways that students relate to one another in college classrooms. This chapter describes a third choice—cooperation among students. Cooperative interaction is the least common but most effective approach for promoting students' learning and teamwork skills.

Cooperation is working together to accomplish shared goals. Within cooperative activities individuals seek outcomes that are beneficial to themselves and to all other group members. *Cooperative learning* is the instructional use of small groups so that students work together to maximize their own and each others' learning (Johnson, Johnson, and Smith, 1991b). Carefully structured cooperative learning involves people working in teams to accomplish a common goal, under conditions that involve both *positive interdependence* (all members must cooperate to complete the task) and both *individual and group accountability* (each member is accountable for the final outcome).

During the past ninety years, nearly six hundred experimental and more than one hundred correlational studies have been conducted comparing the effectiveness of cooperative, competitive, and individualistic efforts. These studies have been conducted by a wide variety of researchers in different decades with different-age subjects, in different subject areas, and in different settings. More is known about the efficacy of cooperative learning than about lecturing, the fifty-minute class period, the use of instructional technology, or almost any other aspect of education. From this research you would expect that the more students work in cooperative learning groups the more they will learn, the better they will understand what they are learning, the easier it will be to remember what they learn, and the better they will feel about themselves, the class, and their classmates.

The multiple outcomes studied can be classified into three major categories: achievement/productivity, positive relationships, and psychological health. Cooperation among students typically results in higher achievement and greater productivity; more caring, supportive, and committed relationships; and greater psychological health, social competence, and self-esteem. A summary of the studies conducted at the higher education level may be found in Johnson, Johnson, and Smith (1991a, 1991b). A comprehensive review of all studies and meta-analyses of their results is available in Johnson and Johnson (1989).

Cooperative learning researchers and practitioners have shown that positive peer relationships are essential to success in college. Isolation and alienation are the best predictors of failure. Two major reasons for dropping out of college are failure to establish a social network of friends and classmates and failure to become academically involved in classes (Tinto, 1994). Working with fellow students, solving problems together, and talking through material together has other benefits as well (McKeachie, Pintrich, Yi-Guang, and Smith, 1986, p. 81): "Student participation, teacher encouragement, and student-student interaction positively relate to improved critical thinking. These three activities confirm other research and theory stressing the importance of active practice, motivation, and feedback in thinking skills as well as other skills. This confirms that discussions . . . are superior to lectures in improving thinking and problem solving." Astin (1992) found that two environmental factors were by far most predictive of positive change in college students' academic development, personal development, and satisfaction. These two factors—*interaction among students and interaction between faculty and students*—carried by far the largest weights and affected more general education outcomes than any other environmental variables studied, including the curriculum content factors.

In short, according to Astin it appears that how students *approach* their general education experiences and how the faculty actually *deliver* the curriculum is far more important than the formal curricular structure. More specifically, the findings strongly support a growing body of research that suggests that one of the crucial factors in the educational development of the undergraduate is the degree to which the student is actively engaged or involved in the undergraduate experience. In his preface to the *Harvard Assessment Seminars: Second Report,* Richard Light (1992, p. 6) came to similar conclusions:

The biggest challenge for me is to ask what the details all add up to. Do the many suggestions that interviewers get from their long conversations with undergraduates drive toward any broad, overarching principle? Is there any common theme that faculty members can use to help students, and indeed that students can use to help themselves? *The answer is a strong yes.* All the specific findings point to, and illustrate, one main idea. It is that students who get the most out of college, who grow the most academically, and who are the happiest, *organize their time to include interpersonal activities with faculty members, or with fellow students, built around substantive, academic work.*

These research findings suggest that curricular planning efforts will reap much-greater payoffs in terms of student outcomes if we focus less on formal structure and content and put much more emphasis on pedagogy and other features of the *delivery system,* as well as on the broader interpersonal and institutional context in which learning takes place.

Types of Cooperative Learning Groups

There are many ways to implement cooperative learning in college classrooms. In terms of the structure continuum, there are informal cooperative learning groups that involve very little structure (typically small, short term, ad hoc groups), informal cooperative learning groups that contain more structure (such as the bookends on a lecture format), formal cooperative learning groups that are highly structured and typically task oriented, and cooperative base groups that are long-term formal groups that are created for student support and encouragement. Each group has a place in providing opportunities for students to be intellectually active and personally interactive both in and outside the classroom. Informal cooperative learning is commonly used in predominately lecture classes and is described in other chapters. Formal cooperative learning can be used in content-intensive classes where the mastery of conceptual or procedural material is essential; however, many faculty find it easier to start in recitation or laboratory sections or to design project courses. Base groups are long-term cooperative learning groups whose principal responsibility is to provide support and encouragement for all their members—that is, to ensure that each member gets the help needed to be successful in the course and in college.

Informal cooperative learning groups are temporary, ad hoc groups that last from a few minutes to one class period. They are used to focus students' attention on the material to be learned, to set a mood conducive to learning, to help organize in advance the material to be covered in a class session, to ensure that students cognitively process the material being taught, and to provide closure to a class session. They are often organized so that students engage in *focused discussions* before and after a lecture, and by interspersing *turn-to-your-partner* discussions throughout a lecture. Informal cooperative learning groups help counter what is proclaimed as the main problem of lectures: that the information passes from the notes of the professor to the notes of the student without passing through the mind of either one.

Base groups are long-term, heterogeneous cooperative learning groups with a stable membership. Their primary responsibility is to provide each student with the support, encouragement, and assistance he or she needs to make academic progress. Base groups personalize the work required and the course learning experiences. These base groups stay the same during the entire course, and longer if possible. The members of base groups should exchange phone numbers and information about schedules because they may wish to meet outside of class. When students have successes, insights, questions, or concerns they wish to discuss they can contact other members of their base group. Base groups typically manage the daily paperwork of the course through the use of group folders, which are typically used by teachers in a cooperative learning class (especially large classes) to communicate with base groups and to manage the flow of paper. During each class period, groups pick up their folder, distribute materials to each individual student—returned assignments, handouts, and so forth—and place new material from students into the folder to be turned in to the teacher.

The focus of this chapter is formal cooperative learning groups, since they are probably the most difficult to implement and have the greatest potential for affecting positive change.

Essential Elements:
What Makes Cooperative Learning Work

Problems that commonly occur when using formal cooperative groups may be minimized by carefully structuring the basic elements. Many faculty who believe they are using cooperative learning are in fact missing its essence. There is a crucial difference between simply putting students in groups to learn and structuring cooperation among students. Cooperation is *not* having students sit side-by-side at the same table to talk with one another as they do their individual assignments. Cooperation is *not* assigning a report to a group of students, on which one student does all the work and the others put their names. Cooperation is *not* having students do a task individually and then having the ones who finish first help the slower students. Cooperation is much more than being physically near other students, discussing material with other students, helping other students, or sharing material among students, although each of these is important in cooperative learning.

To be cooperative a group must have clear, positive interdependence; members must promote each other's learning and success face-to-face, hold each other personally and individually accountable to do a fair share of the work, appropriately use the interpersonal and small-group skills needed for cooperative efforts to be successful, and process as a group how effectively members are working together. These five essential components must be present for small-group learning to be truly cooperative.

Well-structured formal cooperative learning groups are differentiated from poorly structured ones on the basis of the following five essential elements, which should be carefully structured within all levels of cooperative efforts:

1. *Positive interdependence.* The heart of cooperative learning is positive interdependence. Students must believe that they are linked with others in such a way that one cannot succeed unless the other members of the group succeed (and vice versa). Students are working together to get the job done. In other words, students must perceive that they sink or swim together. In formal cooperative learning groups, positive interdependence may by structured by asking group members to agree on an answer for the group (group product-goal interdependence), by making sure that each member can explain the groups' answer (learning goal interdependence), and by fulfilling assigned role responsibilities (role interdependence). Other ways of structuring positive interdependence include having common rewards such as a shared grade (reward interdependence), shared resources (resource interdependence), or a division of labor (task interdependence).

2. *Face-to-face promotive interaction.* Once a professor establishes positive interdependence, he or she must ensure that students interact to help each other accomplish the task and promote one another's success. Students are expected to explain to one another how to solve problems; discuss with one another the nature of the concepts and strategies being learned; teach their knowledge to classmates; explain to one another the connections between present and past learning; and help, encourage, and support each other's efforts to learn. Silent students are uninvolved students who are not contributing to the learning of others or themselves.

3. *Individual accountability/personal responsibility.* The purpose of cooperative learning groups is to make each member a stronger individual in his or her own right. Students learn together so that they can subsequently perform better as individuals. To ensure that each member is strengthened, students are held individually accountable to do their share of the work. The performance of each individual student is assessed and the results given back to the individual and perhaps to the group. The group needs to knows who needs more assistance in completing the assignment, and group members need to know they cannot hitchhike on the work of others. Common ways to structure individual accountability include giving an individual exam to each student, randomly calling on individual students to present their group's answer, and giving an individual oral exam while monitoring groupwork. In the example of a formal cooperative learning lesson provided shortly, individual accountability is structured by requiring each person to learn and teach a small portion of conceptual material to two or three classmates.

4. *Teamwork skills.* Contributing to the success of a cooperative effort requires teamwork skills. Students must have and use the needed leadership, decision-making, trust-building, communication, and conflict-management skills. These skills have to be taught just as purposefully and precisely as academic skills. Many students have never worked cooperatively in learning

situations and therefore lack the needed teamwork skills for doing so effectively. Faculty often introduce and emphasize teamwork skills through assigning differentiated roles to each group member. For example, students learn about the challenge of documenting groupwork by serving as the task recorder; about the importance of developing strategy and talking about how the group is working by serving as process recorder; about providing direction to the group by serving as coordinator; and about the difficulty of ensuring that everyone in the group understands and can explain by serving as the checker.

5.   *Group processing*. Professors need to ensure that members of each cooperative learning group discuss how well they are achieving their goals and maintaining effective working relationships. Groups need to describe what member actions are helpful and unhelpful, and to make decisions about what to continue or change. Such processing enables learning groups to focus on group maintenance, facilitates the learning of collaborative skills, ensures that members receive feedback on their participation, and reminds students to practice collaborative skills consistently. Some of the keys to successful processing are allowing sufficient time for it to take place, making it specific rather than vague, maintaining student involvement in processing, reminding students to use their teamwork skills during processing, and ensuring that clear expectations as to the purpose of processing have been communicated. A common procedure for group processing is to ask each group to list at least three things the group did well and at least one thing that could be improved.

The basic elements of a well-structured formal cooperative learning group are nearly identical to those of high-performance teams in business and industry, as identified by Katzenbach and Smith (1993, p. 45): "A team is a *small number* of people with *complementary skills* who are committed to a *common purpose, performance goals,* and *approach* for which they hold themselves *mutually accountable*" (emphasis in original). Structuring these five essential elements is critical to the success of formal cooperative learning groups. The next section describes in detail how these elements can be structured into such groups.

The Professor's Role in Structuring Formal Cooperative Learning Groups

Before choosing and implementing a formal cooperative learning strategy, several conditions should be evaluated to determine whether or not it is the best approach for the situation. First, is there sufficient time available for students to work in groups both inside and outside the classroom? Second, are the students experienced and skillful enough to manage their work in formal cooperative learning groups? Third, is the task complex enough to warrant a formal group? Fourth, do other instructional goals (such as the development of students' critical thinking skills, higher-level reasoning skills, or teamwork skills) warrant the use of formal cooperative learning groups? If several of these necessary conditions are met, then there is probably sufficient reason to proceed to planning a formal cooperative learning lesson.

Formal cooperative learning groups may last from one class period to several weeks in order to complete specific tasks and assignments—such as learning new conceptual material, engaging in decision making or problem solving, writing a report, conducting a survey or experiment, preparing for an exam, or answering questions or homework problems. Any course requirement may be reformulated to be cooperative. In formal cooperative groups the professor should do the following:

1. *Specify the objectives for the lesson.* In every lesson there should be an academic objective specifying the concepts, strategies, procedures, and so on to be learned, and a teamwork objective specifying the interpersonal or small-group skill to be used and mastered during the lesson.

2. *Make a number of instructional decisions.* The professor has to decide on the size of groups, the method of assigning students to groups, the amount of time that the groups will stay together, the roles the students will be assigned, the materials needed to conduct the lesson, and the way the room will be arranged. Although each of these decisions is complex, some general guidelines may be useful. Further elaboration is available in Johnson, Johnson, and Smith (1991a and 1991b).

First, keep groups small, especially at the beginning. Groups of two or three maximize the involvement and help create a sense of interdependence and accountability. Second, you choose the groups. Random assignment works very well for many faculty. Stratified random groups involve stratifying students along some relevant criterion, such as computing skills or experience, then randomly assigning a student from each category to all the groups. Permitting students to choose their own groups often leads to students working with friends who have a lot of other things to talk about besides the work, and to some students being left out. Third, keep the groups together until the task is completed, and perhaps longer. Changing groups periodically gives students a chance to meet more of their peers and helps them gain skills for quickly getting a group up and running. Fourth, choose roles for group members that are consistent with the requirements of the task and important for smooth group functioning. Many faculty only assign a recorder for the first group assignment, but assigning roles like process recorder, group coordinator, and understanding-checker ensures that all students will have a chance to participate in different roles.

3. *Explain the task and the positive interdependence.* The professor needs to clearly define the assignment, teach the required concepts and strategies, specify the positive interdependence and individual accountability, give the criteria for success, and explain the expected teamwork skill to be engaged in. To make a group project truly cooperative, positive interdependence and individual accountability must be structured in a variety of congruent ways. Positive interdependence is typically structured by asking the group to prepare a single product (goal interdependence), by asking the students to make sure that each person in the group can explain the group's answer (learning goal interdependence), by giving the group one copy of the assignment (resource interdependence), and by assigning a special role to each member (role interdependence).

Individual and group accountability is typically structured by assigning specific functions to each role, randomly calling on individuals to explain their group's answer, monitoring the groups and occasionally asking a student to explain his or her group's answer or method (individual oral exam), asking each member to sign the group's report, and of course, giving individual quizzes, exams, and writing assignments. Courses with extensive formal cooperative learning usually use a combination of group assignments and individual assignments to determine each student's final grade. Typical distributions between individual and group are 95 percent and 5 percent, and 70 percent and 30 percent—that is, between 5 and 30 percent of an individual student's grade is based on groupwork. Some faculty use the groupwork as a baseline or threshold that students must reach, but then they base grades on individual work only. A few faculty in project-based courses base 100 percent of each student's grade on groupwork.

4.   *Monitor students' learning and intervene within the groups to provide task assistance or to increase students' teamwork skills.* The professor systemically observes and collects data on each group as it works. When needed, the professor intervenes to assist students in completing the task accurately and in working together effectively. While students are working, faculty can learn a great deal about what the students know about the material and can often identify problems students are having either with the academic material or working in the group. Typical things to look for include whether they are on-task, the types and qualities of their interactions (What happens when someone says something?), their levels of involvement, the strategy the group is using, and their way of dealing with task or group-functioning difficulties. Teachers either take notes as they circulate among groups or use a checklist to tally types of interactions.

5.   *Evaluate students' learning and help students process how well their group functioned.* Students' learning is carefully assessed and their performances are evaluated. A criteria-referenced evaluation procedure must be used, that is, grading must *not* be curved. Individual students' learning is typically evaluated by written exams, quizzes, and papers. The professor provides time and a structure for members of each learning group to process how effectively they have been working together. A common method for processing is to ask the students to list things they did well while working in the group and things they could improve. A quick process strategy is to ask each individual to list something they did to help the group accomplish its task and one thing they could do even better next time.

Detailed Example of Formal Cooperative Learning

In order for professors to use cooperative learning routinely, they must identify course routines and generic lessons that repeat and structure them cooperatively. Problem-solving, comprehension (read the chapter and answer the questions), jigsaw, structured controversy, and cooperative exams are common examples of repeated practice procedures. Although they are each appropriate in specific contexts, jigsaw is a strategy that permits faculty to help students learn new conceptual material in a format other than lecture or individual reading. Problem-based cooperative learning, used extensively by the author, has been described in numerous references (Smith and Starfield, 1993; Starfield, Smith, and Bleloch, 1994; Woods, 1994; Smith, 1995).

The *cooperative jigsaw strategy* was described by Elliot Aronson in 1978. It is a strategy that highly effective student study groups in content-dense disciplines such as medicine and law have used on an ad hoc basis for many years. The professor's role in a jigsaw involves carefully choosing the material to be jigsawed, structuring the groups and providing them with a clear cooperative context, monitoring to ensure high-quality learning and group functioning, and helping students summarize, synthesize, and integrate the conceptual material. A typical template for a cooperative jigsaw is shown in Exhibit 6.1. The conceptual material you choose for students to learn via a jigsaw strategy should be at a difficultly level that makes the materials accessible; it should be easily divisible into subparts; and it should have some common overriding theme that can be used to integrate the subparts. Students need substantial guidance in working in a jigsaw format. Exhibit 6.2 provides typical guidance given to students to prepare them for working and learning in a jigsaw format.

Many faculty report that the jigsaw approach provides a pleasant alternative to lecture for helping students learn conceptual material, that it helps them "cover" the syllabus, that it helps students learn how to learn and present material, and that it is generally an intense learning experience for the students. Although there is an initial cost of time and coordination to set up the jigsaw, the benefits include students learning more material and remembering it longer, and students learning a procedure that they often start using on their own.

Barriers to Using Cooperative Learning

When faculty have problems (the student who dominates, does not participate, and so on), I typically inquire about and look at the following:

1. Are the groups small (two to three members) and are the members sitting close together?
2. Are positive interdependence and individual accountability structured in multiple ways?
3. Is a criteria-referenced grading procedure being used?

Asking students to cooperate in an environment in which they are being graded on the curve is one of the surest ways to destroy cooperation.

4. Is the professor monitoring the groups, checking on students' understanding of the material and on how well the groups are working?
5. Is there a time and structure for students to process their work in the group?

Exhibit 6.1. Jigsaw Procedure

When you have information you need to communicate to students, an alternative to lecturing is a procedure for structuring cooperative learning groups called *jigsaw* (Aronson, 1978).

Task: Think of a reading assignment you will give in the near future. Divide the assignment into multiple (two to four) parts. Plan how you will use the jigsaw procedure. Script exactly what you will say to the class using each part of the jigsaw procedure. Practice talking students through their role.

Procedure: One way to structure positive interdependence among group members is to use the jigsaw method of creating resource interdependence. The steps for structuring a jigsaw lesson are as follows:

1. *Cooperative groups:* Distribute a set of instructions (see Exhibit 6.2) and materials to each group. The set needs to be divisible into the number of members of the group (two, three, or four parts). Give each member one part of the set of materials.
2. *Preparation pairs:* Assign students the cooperative task of meeting with someone else in the class who is a member of another learning group and who has the same section of the material to complete two tasks:
   a. Learn about and become an expert on the material.
   b. Plan how to teach the material to the other members of the group.
3. *Practice pairs:* Assign students the cooperative task of meeting with someone else in the class who is a member of another learning group and who has learned the same material to share ideas as to how the material may best be taught. These practice pairs review what each person plans to teach their group and how. The best ideas of both are incorporated into each presentation.
4. *Cooperative group:* Assign students the cooperative tasks of
   a. Teaching their area of expertise to the other group members
   b. Learning the material being taught by the other members
5. *Evaluation:* Assess students' degree of mastery of all the material. Recognize those groups in which all members reach the preset criterion of excellence.

Adapted from Johnson, Johnson, and Smith, 1991a.

Exhibit 6.2. The Jigsaw Strategy (Notes to Students)

For this session we are using a procedure for structuring learning groups called *jigsaw*. Each member will be given a different section of the material to be learned. Each member is dependent on the others for success in learning all the material. Each member is accountable for teaching his or her material to the other group members and for learning the material that others teach. The *purposes* of the jigsaw strategy are to

1. Provide an alternative method of introducing new material besides reading and lecture.
2. Create information interdependence among members to increase their sense of mutuality.
3. Ensure that participants orally rehearse and cognitively process the information being learned.
4. Provide an example of high-performance teamwork.

Teaching and Learning Group

Your *task* in this group is to learn all the assigned material. Make sure that each member has a different section and that all sections are covered. Work *cooperatively* to ensure that all group members master all the assigned material.

Preparation to Teach by Pairs

Take one section of the material and find a member of another group who has the same section of the material as you do. Work cooperatively to complete the following tasks:

1. *Learn and become an expert on your material.* Read the material together, discuss it, and master it. Use an active reading strategy (such as *pair reading*):

a. Scan section headings to get an overview of the material.
b. Both persons silently read a paragraph (or short section). Person A summarizes the content to Person B.
c. Person B listens, checks for accuracy, and states how it relates to material previously learned.
d. The two reverse roles and repeat the procedure.

2. *Plan how to teach your material to the other group members.* Share your ideas about how best to teach the material. Make sure your partner is ready.

a. As you read through the material, underline the important points, write questions or ideas in the margins, and add your own thoughts and suggestions.
b. When finished, write down the major ideas and supporting details or examples.
c. Prepare one or more visual aids to help you explain the material.
d. Plan how to make the other members of your group intellectually active rather than passive while they listen to your presentation.

Practice/Consulting Pairs

If you finish the preparation and have time, meet with another person from a different group who is ready and who prepared the same section of the material you did. Work cooperatively to complete the following tasks:

1. Review what each person plans to teach his or her group and share ideas on how to teach the material. Incorporate the best ideas from both plans into each person's presentation.
2. Make sure the other person is ready to teach the material.

Teaching and Learning Group

Meet with your original group and complete the cooperative task of ensuring that all members have mastered all the assigned material by

1. Teaching your area of expertise to the other group members
2. Learning the material being taught by the other group members

The *presenter* should encourage

1. Oral rehearsal
2. Elaboration and integration
3. Implementation ideas

The role of the *listening members* is to

1. Clarify the material by asking appropriate questions.
2. Help the presenter by coming up with novel ways of remembering the important ideas or facts, and to think creatively about the material being presented.
3. Relate the information out loud to previous learned knowledge. Elaborate on the information being presented.
4. Plan out loud how the information can be applied in the immediate future.

Monitoring the Groupwork

Collect some data about the functioning of the group to aid in later group processing. The instructor will also monitor and collect data about the material being learned and about the functioning of the groups.

Evaluation and Processing

The instructor may assess participants' mastery of all the material by giving every participant an exam or by randomly calling on individuals to explain the material they learned.

The instructor will ask each group to process briefly by, for example, asking the group to identify at least one thing that each member did to help other members learn and at least three actions that could be added to improve members learning next time.

Reminder

Remember that learning material in a jigsaw is not a substitute for reading the material on your own later, just as listening to a jigsaw is not a substitute for individual work. The purpose of the jigsaw is to get you involved in the material, to give you an overview, and to try to motivate you to learn more on your own.

Adapted from Aronson, 1978.

Barriers to using cooperative learning can be minimized by starting small and early and then building. Giving students some rationale as to why you are using cooperative learning helps reduce barriers. Providing a variety of forms of cooperative learning and doing something cooperative regularly helps build a habit of cooperation. Carefully monitoring the groups and helping with the problem they are having speeds the progress of cooperative learning. Being patient and positive, and especially having a problem-solving approach, eases the transition to more-cooperative leaning. Finally, working with a colleague to coplan, discuss new ideas, and problem solve makes the transition to cooperative learning much more enjoyable. An extensive discussion of troubleshooting small groups is available in Tiberius (1990).

References

Aronson, E. *The Jigsaw Classroom*. Thousand Oaks, Calif.: Sage, 1978.

Astin, A. *What Matters in College: Four Critical Years Revisited*. San Francisco: Jossey-Bass, 1992.

Johnson, D. W., and Johnson, R. T. *Cooperation and Competition: Theory and Research*. Edina, Minn.: Interaction Book Company, 1989.

Johnson, D. W., Johnson, R. T., and Smith, K. A. *Cooperative Learning: Increasing College Faculty Instructional Productivity*. ASHE-ERIC Higher Education Report No. 4. Washington, D.C.: School of Education and Human Development, George Washington University, 1991a.

Johnson, D. W., Johnson, R. T., and Smith, K. A. *Active Learning: Cooperation in the College Classroom*. Edina, Minn.: Interaction Book Company, 1991b.

Katzenbach, J. R., and Smith, D. K. *The Wisdom of Teams: Creating the High-Performance Organization*. Cambridge, Mass.: Harvard Business School Press, 1993.

Light, R. J. *The Harvard Assessment Seminars: Second Report*. Cambridge, Mass.: Harvard University Graduate School of Education, 1992.

McKeachie, W. J., Pintrich, P. R., Yi-Guang, L., and Smith, D.A.F. *Teaching and Learning in the College Classroom: A Review of the Research Literature*. Ann Arbor: Regents of the University of Michigan, 1986.

Smith, K. A. "Cooperative Learning: Effective Teamwork for Engineering Classrooms." *IEEE Education Society/ASEE Electrical Engineering Division Newsletter*, March 1995, pp. 1–6.

Smith, K. A., and Starfield, A. M. "Building Models to Solve Problems." In J. H. Clarke and A. W. Biddle (eds.), *Teaching Critical Thinking: Reports from Across the Curriculum*. Englewood Cliffs, N.J.: Prentice Hall, 1993.

Starfield, A. M., Smith, K. A., and Bleloch, A. L. *How to Model It: Problem Solving for the Computer Age*. Edina, Minn.: Burgess International Group, 1994.

Tiberius, R. G. *Small Group Teaching: A Trouble-Shooting Guide*. Toronto: OISE Press, 1990.

Tinto, V. *Leaving College: Rethinking the Causes and Cures of Student Attrition* (2nd ed.). Chicago: University of Chicago Press, 1994.

Woods, D. R. *Problem-Based Learning: How to Gain the Most from PBL*. Waterdown, Ontario: Donald R. Woods, 1994.

KARL A. SMITH *is associate professor of civil engineering and associate director for education in the Center for Interfacial Engineering at the University of Minnesota. He is a cooperative learning practitioner.*

Earlier chapters address a broad range of strategies for effectively engaging students in the learning process. While each chapter answers a number of questions about active learning approaches, each also highlights emerging issues in the discussion of involving students in learning.

Emerging Issues in the Discussion of Active Learning

Tracey E. Sutherland

We began this volume by stating that active learning is necessary for achieving many college course objectives and that all faculty can and should use it in their teaching. We also argued that all faculty can develop a repertoire of teaching strategies to actively engage students—strategies that fit their style of teaching and meet course goals effectively. We believe in the necessity of a strong commitment to active learning in the college classroom, and that such a commitment is required to overcome barriers that discourage the use of innovative strategies in the college classroom.

We are certainly not the first educators to suggest that active learning approaches stimulate student learning. Early advocates Maria Montessori and John Dewey recommended that schools begin to include more active and involving teaching approaches. National reports such as the U.S. Department of Education and National Institute of Education's *Involvement in Learning* (Study Group on the Conditions of Excellence in American Higher Education, 1984) and Carnegie Foundation Chairman Ernest Boyer's *College: The Undergraduate Experience in America* (1987) also recommend greater use of active strategies in teaching, and emphasis on students' responsibility for their own learning. Many leaders in higher education use research findings to support their advocacy of active learning. K. Patricia Cross (1987, p. 4) reminds us that "when students are actively involved . . . they learn more than when they are passive recipients of instruction." Alexander Astin (1985, p. 136) tells us that *involvement* is the key: "The amount of student learning and personal development associated with any educational program is directly proportional to the quality and quantity of student involvement in that program." Reviewing the research literature, Bonwell and Eison (1991) provide evidence that active learning strategies strengthen student learning.

So why is it still so difficult? Why are many college faculty still reluctant to incorporate active strategies into their teaching? This chapter explores some of the reasons, as well as some means for overcoming barriers that block more widespread use of active learning in college classrooms. These barriers have foundations deep in basic and long-held assumptions about our roles as teachers in a college environment. It will take the commitment and energy of both faculty members who are educated about the effectiveness of these strategies and administrators who are ready to provide leadership and support to make the changes necessary to provide an educational environment that is supportive of student engagement in the learning process.

Issues of Faculty Evaluation in the Active Learning Classroom

One of the most challenging barriers among those encountered by faculty interested in using active learning is how students and colleagues regard nontraditional approaches. Bonwell and Eison describe this concern as "the greatest barrier of all" (1991, p. 62). One element of the anxiety about students' reception is whether or not they will participate; another is how they might evaluate a course taught in new ways that might require them to learn in new ways. Faculty are also concerned that their peers may disapprove of active learning approaches, considering them less rigorous, not *real* teaching. In this regard, young faculty can be particularly vulnerable. Consider this report of a young assistant professor of biology at a large state university who "conducted her biology class by having the students work in small groups. The class was prepared for the lesson and was comfortable with that strategy. A senior faculty member who was observing the junior faculty member stood up and said, loud enough for all to hear, 'I'll come back when you're teaching'" (Berry, 1989, p. A36). The young professor later received a negative and discouraging evaluation from that colleague, who complained that there was "too much interaction in class" and that she "didn't use the blackboard enough." It is precisely this kind of response that makes using active approaches seem risky to many faculty.

The Risk of Colleagues' Disapproval. It has been said that collaborative peer review should include opportunities for faculty to learn more about teaching effectively, to practice new approaches, to get regular feedback about their teaching performance, and even to have the opportunity to coach each other with the goal of improving teaching (Menges, 1985). Clearly that was not the philosophy in the department of the young faculty member just described. In fact, it is likely that her department had no shared philosophy at all about the kind of teaching performance that *would* receive a positive evaluation.

Faculty evaluation procedures on most college campuses are imperfect and immature (Keig and Waggoner, 1994). Although they typically exist in written form and involve some combination of student ratings, peer evaluation, and administrator evaluation, they do not often address in any depth what is considered on that campus to be "effective teaching." Moreover, if peer observation is a part of the process of collecting evidence, mechanisms for ensuring agreement on what is valued in teaching are rarely in place. This situation is critical to understanding why evaluation procedures present important barriers to faculty interested in using active learning approaches: if active learning's validity can be questioned by colleagues, particularly colleagues who have a role in summative evaluation, few young scholars can risk choosing to use active learning approaches, regardless of their personal commitment or philosophy.

Overcoming the barrier presented by poorly articulated faculty evaluation procedures requires the involvement of senior faculty leaders and support from administrative leaders. Academic departments, led by department chairs and supported by upper-level administration, must take responsibility for developing a shared vision of what acceptable teaching is, and how and by whom it will be measured.

Some promising ideas for making positive changes in evaluation procedures can be found in the literature on the *teaching portfolio* (Seldin, 1991) and in Braskamp and Ory's (1994) discussion of faculty evaluation as *collegial assessment*. If implemented with care, evaluation using teaching portfolios allows faculty to articulate and provide rationales for their chosen teaching approaches. Nonetheless, for the portfolio to function effectively as a tool for evaluation, academic departments must first articulate what will constitute adequate teaching, and then ensure that expectations are clear, both to participating evaluators and to faculty who will be evaluated. Shared values about what constitutes good teaching should be identified, and techniques that encourage students' active engagement should be formally recognized. Departments should consider training portfolio evaluators to assess colleagues, to ensure the reliability of each individual evaluator.

Braskamp and Ory recommend an assessment in which colleagues work together with an emphasis on understanding each other's perspectives, even if one is critiquing and providing feedback to the other. This approach also assumes that faculty have a shared understanding of what constitutes good teaching, and some knowledge of appropriate mechanisms for assessing colleagues and providing constructive feedback. Based on a mentor-style interaction, faculty share syllabi, exams, and classroom materials as well as discussing their teaching philosophies and how those beliefs inform their teaching strategies. On-going opportunities to hear and consider a colleague's rationale for teaching and organizing classes in a certain way give both faculty members the chance to better understand the differences in assumptions and philosophies about teaching that exist between all of us. That understanding is critical to the development of evaluation processes that recognize active learning strategies as legitimate, and an educational environment that encourages innovation in teaching.

The Risk of Student Disapproval. Students also play a definite role in evaluating their classroom experiences. According to Cashin (1988, p. 4), and in polar opposition to much faculty lore, "in general, student ratings tend to be statistically reliable, valid, and relatively free from bias, probably more so than any other data used for faculty evaluation."

An important question about the role of student ratings in the active learning classroom is how these evaluations will be used. Faculty members trying new approaches for the first time make mistakes. In fact, it should be assumed that in the first semester or two some things will not go according to plan. It should also be kept in mind that active learning approaches are often new for students, too. They may not feel comfortable with such approaches, nor confident that they can succeed in the new learning environment. Student evaluations are likely to reflect either scenario. Part of this issue is again tied to departmental and institutional evaluation processes. If feedback from student ratings is used as information to further improve the course, faculty are likely to continue and strengthen their active learning strategies. However, if ratings are used to criticize the teacher and the approach, faculty are likely to withdraw active learning approaches from their repertoire.

In many cases a teacher can take some steps to ease students' transition into a new kind of learning experience. Particularly when using new approaches, it is important to give students frequent opportunities to provide feedback about the class. A simple example is the "one-minute paper" (Angelo and Cross, 1993, p. 148), which uses the last three minutes of the class for students to answer some variation of the following two questions: "What was the most important thing you learned in today's class?" and "What important question(s) remain unanswered?" A variation encouraging feedback on how the class is being taught might be, "What approaches used in today's class facilitated or supported your learning?" or "What approaches got in the way of or prevented your learning?" Student evaluations need not be complex; it is more important for students to feel that their concerns are being heard and considered.

As important as the need to give frequent opportunities for feedback is the need to respond to problems or concerns that arise and are reflected either through feedback surveys or in conversations with students. At times it might make sense to make some changes as a result of student feedback; at other times it might be appropriate to acknowledge students' concerns but then explain your rationale for continuing as planned. Students are more likely to give good evaluations for nontraditional approaches if they understand the instructor's purpose in designing the course to include them.

Creating Positive Classroom Environments

Most college faculty probably feel that the classroom environment is the area of their teaching over which they have the least control. Classroom buildings on most of our campuses are far from new, and recent financial conditions in higher education encourage deferring maintenance on buildings that need it most. Even in newer, well-maintained classroom buildings, environmental structures usually assume the traditional instructional approach: the lecture.

These physical conditions can challenge the professor intent on using active learning strategies.

Although they are perhaps the most obvious element, physical conditions are only one element of the classroom environment. In fact, faculty have a great deal of control over a very important aspect of the environment: the social climate. Classroom environment encompasses both the physical characteristics and the social climate of a learning setting, and structuring a supportive and involving social environment can actually mitigate against some of the difficulties created by limited physical conditions.

Physical Environment. Over the years, many who study college teaching have bemoaned the state of the traditional classroom. Davis (1993, p. 47) notes that "the physical space in which most teaching takes place has been designed with a rather limited idea of what teaching is and with little imagination about what might take place there." A rigid, institutional physical environment encourages student passivity and disconnection. Those who have stood before a half-filled lecture hall with hard seats bolted to the floor in uncompromising rows, trying to maintain eye contact with students scattered in pockets around the room, can attest to the difficulty of connecting with students in such an environment.

While a classroom's physical inadequacies can seem impossible to conquer, faculty committed to using active learning approaches must meet the challenge. This might mean negotiating with a department chair or dean for space more appropriate for participation-based methods. It might involve being willing to teach at different or unusual times of day to have access to more suitable space. Or it could mean taking matters into one's own hands and changing the available space by rearranging it. Sometimes small changes go a long way toward improving a classroom's environment. Opening blinds, changing lighting, moving chairs and tables, and opening or closing doors are small steps that can make a significant difference. Often the challenge is to begin to consider the possibilities of an environment that we have come to take for granted as being limited.

The Social Climate. Interactions and relationships between students and the teacher and among students create the classroom's social climate. Rudolf Moos (1979) describes environments as supportive according to the extent to which people are involved in the setting, support and help each other, and express themselves freely and openly. Reviewing the literature, he reports consistent findings that social climate has a significant effect on a variety of learning outcomes (Moos, 1987). In fact, students are likely to achieve gains on standard achievement tests in classes that have specific academic goals in the context of a supportive classroom climate. In short, while many of us intuitively agree that a pleasant, supportive classroom is a nicer experience, there is evidence that it makes a real difference in students' learning outcomes.

Building a supportive social climate requires establishing expectations that students get to know each other and become accustomed to interacting early in the semester. One common approach is to begin the first class with an icebreaker—for example, pairing students up and asking them to interview their partners. In a smaller class, the pairs can introduce each other to the class. If the class is large, pairs can introduce each other to another pair, then those four students can meet another group of four. This approach works even in a large lecture hall. A professor at Fort Hays State University asks students to prepare a "passport" for her classes. Students use a notecard to make a document that tells something about them. They must include a picture, some information about their likes and dislikes, and something about "where they have been and where they are going." These documents can then be shared with partners or in small groups, or they may be presented by the student to the class (Landrum, 1995). They could also be used to learn students' names more quickly—another strategy for creating a supportive classroom climate.

While interacting with each other is an important first step in developing supportive learning environments, it is also important to consider the expectations and values communicated by the way a class is organized. For example, in *They're Not Dumb, They're Different* (1990, p. 59), Sheila Tobias offers an example of class organization designed to impact social climate—in this case, Dudley Herschbach's chemistry course at Harvard. He works to set a different "mood" in his class, using the social climate as a support to balance the challenges and competitiveness in the typical introductory course. He uses several innovations: he plays popular music as students walk into class, goes to the class early to be available for questions and informal conversation, and meets with an elected "student advisory committee" every two weeks to get regular feedback about how the course is progressing and how students are feeling. He also makes himself available in one of the university's dining halls once a week for conversation with any students who want to come. Over dinner they talk informally about the course and anything else students want to discuss. Herschbach has found that these changes "humanize" the social climate of his introductory chemistry class.

Creating Inclusive Learning Environments. Developing a supportive social climate can have particular benefit for students who come from underrepresented groups. Given that diversity is a fact of life on our campuses today, it is critical that we consider how to provide successful learning experiences for *all* students. There is some evidence that active learning approaches create more productive learning environments for these students.

Adult Learners. On many campuses the majority of students are not the traditional eighteen- to twenty-two-year-olds. Students who are twenty-five or older actually constitute more than 40 percent of today's college population ("The Nation," 1995, p. 19), and these students have unique expectations and needs in the college classroom: they come with a set of life experiences; they are accustomed to being responsible for their own lives, work, and often families; and they expect the classroom experience to *make sense*—to relate to their experience and to be practical either within a career or individual development context. These characteristics make adult learners likely to appreciate and benefit from active learning experiences.

In addressing learning needs for adults, Malcolm Knowles (1980, p. 50) points out that "because adults are themselves richer resources for learning . . . greater emphasis can be placed on techniques that tap their experience . . . such as group discussion, the case method, the critical-incident process, simulation exercises, role playing, skill-practice exercises, [and] field projects." Adult students value the opportunity to apply their hard-won experience in new learning situations. For that reason, Knowles recommends a shift away from transmission-oriented approaches such as the lecture, assigned readings, and prepared presentations toward more participatory and experiential strategies.

Socially and Culturally Diverse Learners. Students from underrepresented social and cultural groups often report that they are at times highly visible in their classes but at other times are overlooked or ignored. Frequently their behavior is scrutinized and generalized to others of their group, while at the same time they are ignored and sometimes excluded from class opportunities. For example, an African-American student in a colleague's composition class recently wrote in a journal assignment of his ambivalence about discussing the racial issues introduced by some of the class readings. On one hand he was very interested in the topic, but on the other hand he felt that if he spoke up in class his comments would be assumed to be true for everyone of his race— or worse, that he would become the spokesperson for his race every time an issue arose. He wrote that he chose to keep silent in the discussion in order to avoid those expectations.

While this feeling of hypervisibility is common, research also shows that students of color, women, and gay and lesbian students are likely to be ignored in their classes, that they are not recognized and encouraged as often as heterosexual male peers, and that they are given fewer opportunities to participate in class (Lopez and Chism, 1993; Sadker and Sadker, 1994; Sandler, 1987). Even faculty who are aware of the literature and personally committed to providing inclusive learning environments often report that they find it difficult to provide equal opportunity for participation within the traditional class setting.

Teaching for Inclusion. Those studying the educational needs of students in underrepresented groups have begun to recommend active learning approaches as important tools for making college classrooms more inclusive. Linda Marchesani and Mauriane Adams (1992, pp. 10–11) have adapted a model that describes four dimensions to be considered in thinking about teaching and learning issues in socially and culturally diverse classes. They recommend that faculty (1) know their students in order to understand the ways students from different backgrounds experience the college classroom; (2) know themselves as a person with a history of socialization in academe and a particular cultural background with its own learned beliefs; (3) create course content that incorporates diverse social and cultural perspectives; and (4) develop a repertoire of teaching methods that effectively address learning styles of students from diverse social and cultural backgrounds. Teaching effectively means not only learning about underrepresented students' backgrounds and expectations but also developing alternative teaching methods to better include those students in the learning experience.

Numerous studies suggest that inclusive classrooms employ the following: collaborative projects that balance individual and group performance expectations; group assignments that combine students of different social and cultural groups, ages, and genders; class activities that build peer relationships; opportunities for demonstrations or dramatic presentations; simulations and role-plays; and other, similar methods. Using approaches that concentrate on engaging *all* students can eliminate concern about whether a particular student or group of students is participating (Anderson and Adams, 1992; Pierson, Shavlick, and Touchton, 1989; Sandler, Silverberg, and Hall, 1996). At the same time, deliberate steps must still be taken to structure those activities to ensure *equitable* participation. In their new report, Sandler, Silverberg, and Hall (1996) recommend the use of cooperative learning strategies to ensure more equitable participation in class. However, they point out that using active learning approaches does not necessarily guarantee that women students, students of color, non-traditional-aged students, or gay and lesbian students will truly have equal opportunity to participate. Unless steps are taken to design a course and its assignments to ensure that each student participates equally and to create a sense of community responsibility for making certain that everyone participates and learns, majority students, particularly male students, will likely dominate even active learning experiences.

Meeting the needs of diverse classrooms requires good understanding and preparation. While it is clear that active learning approaches are a good tool for meeting some of these students' learning needs, there are also other important issues to take into account in creating truly inclusive classroom learning environments.

The Role of Active Learning in the Discussion of Assessment

While future employers, parents, and educators agree that the skills and attitudes developed through active learning experiences are critical to students' future success, far less attention has been paid to assessing those abilities than to assessing content-knowledge and academic skills (RiCharde, Olney, and Erwin, 1993). Books and articles encouraging the adoption of active and cooperative learning strategies describe their effectiveness in developing students' communication skills, leadership abilities, ethical decision making, and critical thinking and self-assessment skills, but they do not address the *assessment* of those skills (Bonwell and Eison, 1991; Halpern and Associates, 1994; Johnson, Johnson, and Smith, 1991; Meyers and Jones, 1993). If these outcomes are truly important, why are they rarely included in conversations about institutional assessment?

Institutional-Level Assessment. Those involved in the institutional assessment movement often contend that "we measure what we treasure," and in the college classroom what we have treasured is *content*. Certainly we would all agree that mastering disciplinary knowledge and modes of inquiry are a central part of a student's college education. However, the mission statements of most colleges also make claims of developing skills beyond content objectives. Those statements are full of rhetoric about developing good citizens with strong leadership abilities and excellent communication skills, who appreciate diversity and respect other cultures, make ethical decisions, and serve their communities. However, neither institution-level assessment initiatives nor individual course assessments typically include evaluation of these kinds of skills.

Institution-level assessment initiatives are typically designed to establish accountability. While their goal is to evaluate student learning outcomes, most campuses are more interested in outcomes of the general education curriculum or the major and as such concentrate primarily on achievements in content mastery. A couple of exceptions are Alverno College and Truman State University (formerly Northeast Missouri State University). At Alverno, content and noncontent outcomes are combined. For example, an assessment outcome for chemistry majors is the ability to use the "methodology and models of chemistry to define and solve problems independently" and to do so "collaboratively." Business majors are asked to demonstrate that they can "use organizational and management theory to interact effectively in organizational contexts that require leadership of groups or other types of interpersonal interaction" (Loacker and Mentkowski, 1993, pp. 7–8). Truman State University uses student portfolios to assess general education outcomes, focusing on student gains in such areas as interdisciplinary thinking, aesthetic analysis, and growth as a thinker. These desired outcomes move beyond strict content objectives to address skills students need for success in future work and life.

While many institutions are developing assessment approaches that can address noncontent outcomes, approaches such as portfolios and interviews (Black, 1993; Fong, 1988; Greenberg, 1988, Magruder and Young, 1995; RiCharde, Olney, and Erwin, 1993) still focus primarily on content objectives or indicators of student satisfaction with various aspects of their college experience.

Classroom-Level Assessment. The reasons that faculty find it difficult to assess noncontent outcomes are the same as the reasons they find it difficult to consider using new teaching approaches. Faculty are experts in their field of study. They have spent their professional lives developing skill and confidence in their abilities as chemists, sociologists, rhetoricians, and art historians. Their training and focus has been on content, and few have been supervised or mentored in teaching and evaluating students.

Although lack of experience and a tradition valuing the attainment of knowledge focus faculty interest on assessing students' content knowledge, many faculty do expect students to develop other skills in their courses. When this is true, those skills should be addressed in the course, and students' achievement should be explicitly evaluated. For example, if one objective of a group project in a psychology class is that students will learn to deliver poised professional presentations, then that objective should be shared with the class, and students should receive feedback on their level of accomplishment of that outcome and an evaluation of their performance. If that objective is assumed to be implicit but significant attention is given only to discussing the content issues inherent in the project, then students will have every reason to assume that the content objective is more important. This is a missed teachable moment. Students generally know that they are supposed to learn speaking skills in college. However, they do not always realize the importance of speaking skills in the working world. This kind of project could present an opportunity to address the importance of that skill and the reason for its inclusion in the course. Without a good understanding of the importance of noncontent objectives, students will spend their time on the objectives that *have* been articulated—the content objectives.

The assessment movement is young and just reaching the point of having enough campuses participating at sufficient levels to begin understanding its emerging issues. As higher education continues its work toward demonstrating how colleges and universities make a difference, the importance of addressing the development of noncontent outcomes will continue to gain attention.

Using Electronic Tools: Some Benefits and Challenges

The use of e-mail, electronic conferencing, and the Internet in teaching is a hot topic, both in the literature and on the listservs (electronic discussion groups) in higher education, and faculty on most campuses are demanding to know more about these approaches. It is a good sign that many of these tools encourage students to be actively engaged in learning (see Chapter Five). While faculty enthusiasm is exciting, new demands on already-stretched resources bring new challenges to administrative decision makers. As faculty become increasingly interested in these approaches, an important question is whether the hardware and services available on most campuses will be adequate to meet their needs.

Limited Availability of Resources and Support. Steven Gilbert (1995) quotes Dickens in describing the challenges of supporting technological growth at this time in higher education: it is the best of times and the worst of times. There has never been a greater array of options available for developing technological infrastructures, nor greater interest in expanding the potential of those options. At the same time, the range of student and faculty needs is expanding beyond even experts' experience, at a time when competition for resources is fierce.

Technology is only as effective as those who use it, and without adequate training and support even interested faculty cannot successfully incorporate electronic tools into their teaching toolbox. It is often assumed that once faculty get new hardware they will easily and quickly be able to change their teaching approaches to take advantage of the technology. Thus, funds to provide support for faculty and staff as they upgrade their skills are rarely included in technology budgets (Ehrmann, 1995). As a result, most campuses are experiencing critical shortages of technical support staff at a time when interest is on the rise. Faculty determined to use technology-assisted active learning strategies may need to seek support from more experienced colleagues in order to learn new skills and ideas for using technology in teaching.

Rewards for the Struggle. Although the barriers to progress on some fronts are significant, basic electronic tools are available on many campuses to virtually everyone, allowing students, faculty, and staff to access the Internet, use e-mail, and participate in electronic conferences. When these tools are in place, and with an initial commitment of time, most faculty can consider using them to encourage active learning in their classes.

Those who have already done so report positive results, particularly among students who are not typically active in the classroom itself. These approaches may offer particular promise for overcoming barriers of bias; all students have equal access and opportunity for involvement. In many classes the motivation level of the entire class is enhanced by using electronic tools. For example, faculty using electronic conferencing in foreign language classes find that students appreciate the access and flexibility of the conference as opposed to a language lab and enjoy actually *using* the language to converse with fellow students. Without the pressure of time or concern with accent and pronunciation, students can relax and concentrate on interpreting messages and developing their replies. At least one study has shown that students participating in electronic conferencing in foreign language classes also excel in oral performance in class (Ehrmann, 1995).

While they offer encouraging opportunities for incorporating active learning in college classes, the electronic tools addressed in this volume represent only one small element of the larger conversation about technology in higher education. Questions related to such issues as developing adequate institutional infrastructure, increasing information literacy, and creating hypermedia for teaching are connected by similar concerns of adequate resources and services. The future will bring many challenges for those using technology in their teaching and those working to support them, but it will also hold many opportunities for creative solutions.

Conclusion

These barriers to wider use of active learning are not insurmountable, but overcoming them will require change—change that will involve challenging some of our basic assumptions about teaching and learning processes. Given the evidence that active learning strategies are necessary for achieving many learning outcomes, we must begin to work together to find ways to make those changes.

Parker Palmer says that teaching and learning are communal activities that "require a continual cycle of discussion, disagreement, and consensus over what has been seen and what it all means" (1987, p. 25). That conversation requires productive conversation between students and faculty, among faculty, and between faculty and administrative colleagues. It will take the commitment, energy, and leadership of faculty who are educated about and determined to use active learning approaches, of students who understand and are committed to the goals of active learning, and of administrators who are prepared to provide support and leadership to make the kind of changes we need to create learning environments that better support student engagement in the learning process.

References

Anderson, J. A., and Adams, M. "Acknowledging the Learning Styles of Diverse Student Populations: Implications for Instructional Design." In L.L.B. Border and N.V.N. Chism (eds.), *Teaching for Diversity*. New Directions for Teaching and Learning, no. 49. San Francisco: Jossey-Bass, 1992.

Angelo, T. A., and Cross, K. P. *Classroom Assessment Techniques: A Handbook for College Teachers* (2nd ed.). San Francisco: Jossey-Bass, 1993.

Astin, A. W. *Achieving Educational Excellence: A Critical Assessment of Priorities and Practices in Higher Education*. San Francisco: Jossey-Bass, 1985.

Berry, E. "Newly Hired Young Scholars Should be Nurtured, Not Resented." *Chronicle of Higher Education*, June 21, 1989, p. A36.

Black, L. C. "Portfolio Assessment." In T. Banta (ed.), *Making a Difference: Outcomes of a Decade of Assessment in Higher Education*. San Francisco: Jossey-Bass, 1993.

Bonwell, C. C., and Eison, J. A. *Active Learning: Creating Excitement in the Classroom*. ASHE-ERIC Higher Education Report No. 1. Washington, D. C.: George Washington University, School of Education and Human Development, 1991.

Boyer, E. L. *College: The Undergraduate Experience in America*. New York: HarperCollins, 1987.

Braskamp, L. A., and Ory, J. C. *Assessing Faculty Work: Enhancing Individual and Institutional Work*. San Francisco: Jossey-Bass, 1994.

Cashin, W. E. "Student Ratings of Teaching: A Summary of the Research." *Idea Paper No. 20*. Manhattan: Kansas State University, Center for Faculty Evaluation and Development, 1988.

Cross, K. P. "Teaching for Learning." *AAHE Bulletin*, 1987, 39, 3–7.

Davis, J. R. *Better Teaching, More Learning: Strategies for Success in Postsecondary Settings*. Phoenix, Ariz.: Oryx Press, 1993.

Ehrmann, S. C. "Asking the Right Questions." *Change*, 1995, 27 (2), 20–27.

Fong, B. "Assessing the Departmental Major." In J. H. McMillan (ed.), *Assessing Students' Learning*. New Directions for Teaching and Learning, no. 34. San Francisco: Jossey-Bass, 1988.

Gilbert, S. W. "Teaching, Learning, and Technology." *Change*, 1995, 27 (2), 47–52.

Greenberg, K. L. "Assessing Writing: Theory and Practice." In J. H. McMillan (ed.), *Assessing Students' Learning*. New Directions for Teaching and Learning, no. 34. San Francisco: Jossey-Bass, 1988.

Halpern, D. F., and Associates. *Changing College Classrooms: New Teaching and Learning Strategies for an Increasingly Complex World*. San Francisco: Jossey-Bass, 1994.

Johnson, D. W., Johnson, R. T., and Smith, K. A. *Active Learning: Cooperation in the College Classroom*. Edina, Minn.: Interaction Book Company, 1991.

Keig, L., and Waggoner, M. D. *Collaborative Peer Review: The Role of Faculty in Improving College Teaching*. ASHE-ERIC Higher Education Report No. 2, 1994. Washington, D.C.: George Washington University, School of Education and Human Development, 1994.

Knowles, M. S. *The Modern Practice of Adult Education: From Pedagogy to Andragogy*. River Grove, Ill.: Follett, 1980.

Landrum, M. S. "Techniques for Learning Students' Names." Paper developed from solicited contributions on the POD Network listserv, Spring 1995.

Loacker, G., and Mentkowski, M. "Creating a Culture Where Assessment Improves Learning." In T. Banta (ed.), *Making a Difference: Outcomes of a Decade of Assessment in Higher Education*. San Francisco: Jossey-Bass, 1993.

Lopez, G., and Chism, N. "Classroom Concerns of Gay and Lesbian Students: The Invisible Minority." *College Teaching*, 1993, *41* (3), 97–103.

Magruder, J. W., and Young C. C., "Junior Interview Project on Teaching and Learning." In T. W. Banta (ed.), *Assessment in Practice: Putting Principles to Work on College Campuses*. San Francisco: Jossey-Bass, 1995.

Marchesani, L. S., and Adams, M. "Dynamics of Diversity in the Teaching-Learning Process: A Faculty Development Model for Analysis and Action." In M. Adams (ed.), *Promoting Diversity in College Classrooms: Innovative Responses for the Curriculum, Faculty, and Institutions*. New Directions for Teaching and Learning, no. 52. San Francisco: Jossey-Bass, 1992.

Menges, R. J. "Career-Span Faculty Development." *College Teaching*, 1985, *35*, 181–184.

Meyers, C., and Jones, T. B. *Promoting Active Learning: Strategies for the College Classroom*. San Francisco: Jossey-Bass, 1993.

Moos, R. *Evaluating Educational Environments*. San Francisco: Jossey-Bass, 1979.

Moos, R. "Person-Environment Congruence in Work, School, and Health Care Settings." *Journal of Vocational Behavior*, 1987, *31*, 231–247.

"The Nation: Students." *Chronicle of Higher Education*, September 1, 1995, p. 19.

Palmer, P. J. "Community, Conflict, and Ways of Knowing." *Change*, 1987, *19* (5), 20–25.

Pierson, C. S., Shavlick, D. L., and Touchton, J. G. (eds.). *Educating the Majority: Women Challenge Tradition in Higher Education*. New York: American Council on Education/Macmillan, 1989.

RiCharde, R. S., Olney, C. A., and Erwin, T. D. "Cognitive and Affective Measures of Student Development." In T. Banta (ed.), *Making a Difference: Outcomes of a Decade of Assessment in Higher Education*. San Francisco: Jossey-Bass, 1993.

Sadker, M., and Sadker, D. *Failing at Fairness*. New York: Scribner, 1994.

Sandler, B. R., Silverberg, L. A., and Hall, R. M. *The Chilly Classroom Climate: A Guide to Improve the Education of Women*. Washington D.C.: National Association for Women in Education, 1996.

Sandler, B. "The Classroom Climate: Still a Chilly One for Women?" In C. Lasser (ed.), *Educating Men and Women Together: Coeducation in a Changing World*. Champaign: University of Illinois Press, 1987.

Seldin, P. *The Teaching Portfolio*. Bolton, Mass.: Anker Publishing, 1991.

Study Group on the Conditions of Excellence in American Higher Education. *Involvement in Learning: Realizing the Potential of American Higher Education*. Washington, D.C.: National Institute of Education/U.S. Department of Education, 1984.

Tobias, S. *They're Not Dumb, They're Different: Stalking the Second Tier*. Tucson, Ariz.: Research Corporation, 1990.

TRACEY E. SUTHERLAND is director of faculty development at Truman State University (formerly Northeast Missouri State University), Kirksville, Missouri.

INDEX

Ordering Information

NEW DIRECTIONS FOR TEACHING AND LEARNING is a series of paperback books that presents ideas and techniques for improving college teaching, based both on the practical expertise of seasoned instructors and on the latest research findings of educational and psychological researchers. Books in the series are published quarterly in Spring, Summer, Fall, and Winter and are available for purchase by subscription as well as by single copy.

SUBSCRIPTIONS cost $52.00 for individuals (a savings of 35 percent over single-copy prices) and $79.00 for institutions, agencies, and libraries. Please do not send institutional checks for personal subscriptions. Standing orders are accepted. Prices subject to change. (For subscriptions outside of North America, add $7.00 for shipping via surface mail or $25.00 for air mail. Orders *must be prepaid* in U.S. dollars by check drawn on a U.S. bank or charged to VISA, MasterCard, or American Express.)

SINGLE COPIES cost $20.00 plus shipping (see below) when payment accompanies order. California, New Jersey, New York, and Washington, D.C., residents please include appropriate sales tax. Canadian residents add GST and any local taxes. Billed orders will be charged shipping and handling. No billed shipments to post office boxes. (Orders from outside North America *must be prepaid* in U.S. dollars by check drawn on a U.S. bank or charged to VISA, MasterCard, or American Express.)

SHIPPING (SINGLE COPIES ONLY): $10.00 and under, add $2.50; to $20.00, add $3.50; to $50.00, add $4.50; to $75.00, add $5.50; to $100.00, add $6.50; to $150.00, add $7.50; over $150.00, add $8.50.

DISCOUNTS FOR QUANTITY ORDERS are available. Please write to the address below for information.

ALL ORDERS must include either the name of an individual or an official purchase order number. Please submit your order as follows:
    Subscriptions: specify series and year subscription is to begin
    Single copies: include individual title code (such as TL54)

MAIL ALL ORDERS TO:
    Jossey-Bass Publishers
    350 Sansome Street
    San Francisco, CA 94104-1342

FOR SUBSCRIPTION SALES OUTSIDE OF THE UNITED STATES, CONTACT:
    any international subscription agency or Jossey-Bass directly.